Part-Time Employment for the Low-Income Elderly

Issues in Aging
(Vol. 6)
Garland Reference Library of Social Science
(Vol. 1016)

Issues in Aging

Diana K. Harris, Series Editor

Part-Time Employment for the Low-Income Elderly
Experiences from the Field

Leslie B. Alexander
Lenard W. Kaye

GARLAND PUBLISHING, INC.
New York & London
1997

Library of Congress Cataloging-in-Publication Data

Alexander, Leslie B.
        Part-time employment for the low-income elderly : experiences
from the field / by Leslie B. Alexander and Lenard W. Kaye.
                p.   cm. — (Garland reference library of social science ; v.
1016. Issues in aging ; v. 6)
        Includes bibliographical references and index.
        ISBN 0-8153-1976-2 (alk. paper)
        1. Aged—Employment—United States. 2. Part-time
empoyment—United States.   I. Kaye, Lenard W. II. Title. III.
Series: Garland reference library of social science ; v. 1016. IV. Series:
Garland reference library of social science ; v. 1016. IV. Series: Garland reference library of social science. Issues in aging ; v. 6.
        HD6280.A449 1997
        331.3'98—dc20   96-35889
                                                                        CIP

Printed on acid-free, 250-year-life paper
Manufactured in the United States of America

Contents

List of Tables

Series Editor's Preface

This series attempts to address the topic of aging from a wide variety of perspectives and to make available some of the best gerontological thought and writing to researchers, professional practitioners, and students in the field of aging as well as in other related areas. All the volumes in the series are written and/or edited by outstanding scholars and leading specialists on current issues of considerable interest.

Based on interviews and case records, this study of low-income older persons who hold part-time jobs fills an important gap in research about the work experiences of this segment of our population. Although part-time work for the elderly persons studied has both negative and positive consequences, the authors conclude that overall the positive aspects far outweighed the negative ones. This book makes an important contribution toward furthering our understanding of part-time jobs in general and serves as a valuable resource for knowledge about low-income elderly workers in particular.

Diana K. Harris
University of Tennessee

Foreword

One quality dominates thinking about our society today—change—its rapidity, its multifaceted nature, and the complexity of interactions it causes that motivate policy responses in both the public and private spheres. In our striving for the American ideal of a satisfying and ever-rising standard of living, we are constantly confronted by changes in demographics and in labor force composition, technological developments, industrial and occupational characteristics, and organization of work within an enterprise. These are all molded by changes in national and international economic and political circumstances.

Changes of this nature require adaptations in our work and values, as well as reassessment of data and reinterpretation and reevaluation of economic, political, and work organization events and institutional behavior. Yet we always seem to lag behind in our understanding and adapting to these new circumstances, both individually and in social policies. Nowhere is this phenomenon more evident than in discussions about the nature, structure, and role of work in our lives and in successful business functioning.

Professors Alexander and Kaye make an important contribution to our thinking about work in their inquiry into the work lives of one group in the population—low-income elderly, ages 55 and over. Currently working part time, the majority in subsidized low-skill jobs, they are a population group growing in national importance, increasing in healthy longevity, and often in need of some supplementation to retirement income. About 40 percent of the respondents in the study, for example, had no income other than Social Security, a social benefit that since its inception has never been conceived of as more than a minimum base upon which to build income adequacy.

Part-time work, work of less than 35 hours a week, is not new. Nearly one-fifth of all nonagricultural employees work part time. Although the numbers in part-time work have increased between 1969 and 1993 (from 10.8 to 20.7 million persons), the proportion of workers in part-time work has increased only slightly—from 15.5 to 18.8 percent (Snider, 1995, 239). On the other hand, almost all of the increase in part-time workers since 1973 has been due to an increased rate of growth of involuntary part-time workers, that is, those who would have preferred a full-time job (Nardone, 1995, 283). In 1989, for example, nearly one-fourth of all part-time workers were involuntary part-timers. By 1993, involuntary part time had grown from 4.3 percent of employment (1989) to 5.5 percent (Mishel and Bernstein, 1994, 219).

Such a trend raises questions about the preference for and quality of opportunities available in part-time jobs. In general, the supply of part-time workers reflects particular interests of the major groups that work part time—women, teenagers, and the elderly. Supply side reasons for part-time work among the elderly are well detailed in the research findings to be discussed later. The demand for part-time workers has certainly increased, partly reflecting a shift in the industrial and occupational composition of work from manufacturing to services and retail trade, where 29 percent and 41 percent of workers, respectively, work part time compared with 5.8 percent in manufacturing (Snider, 1995, 241). Between 1979 and 1989, roughly three-fourths of new jobs created were in these two industries (Mishel and Bernstein, 1994, 222–23), which account for about 60 percent of part-time workers (Snider, 1995, 241). In addition, interest in part-time labor on the part of business has been spurred by global competition, downsizing, and technological developments that have been reflected in an intensified interest in work flexibility, minimization of labor costs, and use of contingent labor, of which part-time work is a major component. Thus, part-time work opportunities exist. The important question is whether elders are interested in working in these part-time jobs and, if so, do these jobs fulfill their needs and at the same time meet the needs of the employing enterprise? This is a key question to which the Alexander and Kaye investigation makes a significant contribution.

Elderly workers constitute a special group in the population.

Although the number of elderly over age 65 has grown from 8.1 percent to 12.5 percent of the population between 1950 and 1990, the proportion of elderly in the labor force is low and has been declining in recent years. Most workers appear to retire as soon as they can afford to (Schulz, 1988, in Rix, 1996, 7). In 1992, for example, between ages 55 and 64 women's labor force participation rate was 46.6 percent; over age 65, it was only 8.3 percent. For men, the labor force participation rate was 67 percent between ages 55 and 64, but only 16.2 percent for the group over age 65. Moreover, in 1992, of the 4.6 million employees ages 65 and over, a significant proportion, 56.3 percent, worked part time (Snider, 1995, 242). For elders who work, low wages are prevalent. Twenty-seven percent of all hourly wage earners ages 55 and over were minimum wage workers in 1993; the proportion was over two-thirds for female hourly workers. Over two-thirds of minimum wage workers (compared with one-fourth of all hourly wage earners) are employed part time (Rix, 1996, 7). Yet one analysis shows an increase in part-time work between 1984 and 1993 among retirees, at least among men younger than age 65 (Herz, 1995). Whatever the explanation for retirement trends, data indicates that opportunities for gradual retirement, accompanied by part-time work in one's regular job, are rare (Ferber, 1996, 5). Labor force attachment of the elderly in other jobs is often associated with financial necessity (Rix, 1996, 7).

All of these comments document the importance of the Alexander and Kaye survey for gaining insight into the views and experience of elderly, low-income, part-time workers. The brief overview here is developed and expanded upon in chapters 1 and 2. Standing on their own, these chapters provide an excellent general survey and review of national trends relating to work in the United States in the recent past. At the same time, they give a context for and introduction to the more specific investigation of this study.

The study focus was chosen partly to fill a gap in data on part-time employment, which is sparse for low-income elderly and especially for women and minorities, and partly to assess the value of this work structure that in the literature is both praised as providing financial support and a transition to retirement and criticized for its low wages, few benefits, and general status as a less relevant work structure, engaged in with less commitment. Thus, the study group, unskilled and semiskilled workers, the majority in subsidized jobs in the Philadelphia area, consists of contigent workers, ages 55 and over, two-thirds of whom are women, and almost two-thirds minorities.

The authors seek to explore the structure and qualities of this part-time work, the expectations about its value to elders, and their actual work experiences that have contributed to or detracted from their work satisfaction. Were these aspects similar for all interviewees or do they reflect differences among them? What was the relationship to past work experience and to the job placement agency? In sum, does part-time work on balance offer something positive for this group of elderly low-income workers? Can part-time jobs be "good" jobs? What function can they serve for low-income elderly, many of whom are women and minorities?

Given this general framework, chapters 3, 4, and 5 set the stage for the analysis by describing the methodology and the characteristics of the sample. Chapter 3, "Our Approach to Learning about Low-Income Older Adults Who Worked Part-Time," describes the study's three-sided research approach, which involves case record analysis, participant interviews, and interviews with program directors and staff members at the four study sites.

Chapter 4, "Who Were the Low-Income Older Part-Timers?", describes in detail the 613 program participants and 265 interview respondents, a majority of whom had at least a high school education but whose median income was near or below poverty level.

Chapter 5, "The Previous Work Careers of Part-Time and Unemployed Elders," based on interviews only, both describes the general work affiliation of part-timers in their longest or "career" job and also compares them with the group of unemployed at the time of their interviews, a group who are described in more detail later in the book.

Chapters 6, 7, and 8 describe the job placement and the structure and function of the part-time jobs held. Chapter 6, "Job Placement Services and the Older Worker," using both records and interview data, describes the workers' placements. Chapter 7, "The Structural Characteristics of Part-Time Work," based on interview data only, describes the jobs and work schedules in greater detail. Chapter 8, "The Functional Characteristics of Part-Time Work," provides interviewee descriptions of the quality of the jobs held.

Chapters 9, 10, and 11, like chapters 7 and 8, analyze interviewees' responses for those still working part time at the time of the interview. These chapters further elucidate attitudes about job satisfaction (chapter 9), discrimination (chapter 10), and work and retirement (chapter 11). Relatively high levels of job satisfaction were reported by interviewees, with close to 60 percent of the variance in job satisfaction scores explained by ability to use existing skills, better fringe benefits, positive attitudes towards elders by supervisors and others, desirable work schedules, and minority status.

The two chapters preceding the concluding one report on two special cases: identified members of the interviewee group who had been placed in part-time positions in fiscal 1987 but who were unemployed at the time of the interview about two years later (chapter 12) and the small group of elders placed by one of the agencies, who were working full time at the time of the interview (chapter 13). Findings are summarized in each chapter.

Alexander and Kaye in their final chapter, chapter 14, "Conclusions and Recommendations," conclude that the part-time jobs of the group of elderly studied displayed both good and bad characteristics. From the standpoint of wages the jobs were mostly "bad" ones, in 1985 paying a somewhat lower median hourly wage than that for all part-time workers. Hours worked additional to those of their regular schedule were either not compensated or were paid at regular rather than overtime hourly rates. Fringe benefits were low. On the other hand, there were a number of "good" compensating aspects of their jobs. Most elders obtained the kind of position they sought—to provide some income and to keep busy. They were placed in steady, nonseasonal jobs with predictable work hours that made use of their skills. They received satisfaction from their interactions with other workers. On the other hand, a relatively high rate of unemployment only two years post-placement was noted, as were some racial/ethnic differences in labor market experiences. In their recommendations for further policy development, the authors deplore the general lack of formal training or retooling by the placement agencies. On balance, however, it seems that, although not without problems, the experience was a positive one for elder low-income part-timers, including the fact, for some, of having subsidized jobs. Alexander and Kaye would like to see the expansion of further support and education and training for this group of low-income elders go forward together. They feel that there are benefits for employers and for society as much as for elders who find a supportive and contributing niche for their later years.

To all of this, this writer says "Amen." I find part-time work to be a several-sided prism, acknowledged in other literature but never described so thoroughly as here based on the expressed views of a group of low-income elders themselves. We know that all is not well with the earnings and benefits levels associated with part-time work, with its sometimes exploitative application within the work world, and with women's disadvantaged rewards in the market relative to those of men. We know that more research is needed, both the analysis and interpretation of available large-scale data series and interviews with those working within a part-time framework and covering not only elders but also other age and racial and ethnic groups.

This study adds to our understanding of the role part-time work can play by putting flesh on the bones of more general conceptualization and data analysis. It documents the positive attributes that are perceived for part-time work by those who are engaged in it, while other groups and individuals address its inequities and inadequacies. We need to build on this base of positive information. We need to reappraise part-time work and adjust its reward level to reflect an equality, pro-rated with that for an equivalent level of productivity in full-time work. We need to consider a new conception of work organization, its distinguishing characteristics now being defined and tested in a collaborative project of one large corporation and a research group centered at the Massachusetts Institute of Technology (MIT) (Bailyn, et al. 1996). In its essence, the project seeks changes in work practices that affect both work and family lives with mutual benefit to the organization and to employees. Both flexibility and support in workplace structures and culture are the means to this end, embracing part-time as well as other work rhythms. Elders, as well as others, should benefit from the greater range and flexibility in the way work can be carried on.

Moreover, studies such as the Alexander and Kaye study, which demonstrate positive aspects for elders of part-time jobs even in the face of some negatives in the work itself, are beginning to have a parallel in studies that address issues of interest to employers about the value of employing elders in full- or part-time jobs. They document the strong work motivation and the productive efficiency that can result (AARP, 1995a; AARP, 1995b; Davis, 1994; Phillion & Burgger, 1994), but also point out several potential areas of performance weakness (e.g., difficulties in adapting to change) that can be present. Most important, we need to develop public and private sector policies for training and retraining elders to enhance their job opportunities and ensure that offered skills respond to workplace needs. Professors Alexander and Kaye provide us with a basic building block of first-hand information and data analysis for understanding the role that part-time work can play for elders wanting to participate in the work world. This work can provide a model for moving forward with further studies and with policy design to ensure evolution of this employment structure so that it better meets the needs of all worker and employer groups.

Hilda Kahne
Professor of Economics
Heller Graduate School for
Advanced Studies in Social Welfare
Brandeis University

Note

Data with no cited source are taken from the book.

References

American Association of Retired Persons. *American Business and Older Workers: A Road Map to the 21st Century.* 1995a.

American Association of Retired Persons. *Valuing Older Workers: A Study of Costs and Productivity.* 1995b.

Bailyn, Lotte, Rapoport, Rhona, Kolb, Deborah , and Fletcher, Joyce, et al. "Rethinking Work and Family: A Catalyst for Organizational Change." Working Paper 3892–96, Cambridge, MA: MIT, Sloan School of Management, April 1996.

Davis, Trudi Jo. "Breaking the Age Barrier." *Secure Retirement* 3, No. 2 (March 1994): 20–22.

Ferber, Marianne, and Waldfogel, Jane. *Contingent Work.* Cambridge, MA: Radcliffe Public Policy Institute, 1996.

Herz, Diane E. "Work After Early Retirement: An Increasing Trend Among Men." *Monthly Labor Review* 118, No. 4 (April 1995): 13–20.

Mishel, Lawrence, and Bernstein, Jarod. *The State of Working America, 1994–95.* New York: M.E. Sharpe, 1994.

Phillion, Lee, and Burgger, John R. "Encore! Retirees Give Top Performance as Temporaries." *HR Magazine* 39, No. 10 (Oct. 1994): 74–77.

Rix, Sara "Protecting Workers at the Bottom: The Minimum Wage and America's Minimum Wage Workers." Washington, DC: AARP Issue Brief Number 25, 1996:5.

Schulz, James H. "Job Matching in an Aging Society: Barriers to the Utilization of Older Workers." Paper prepared for the Annual Meeting of the Gerontology Society of America. San Francisco, November 1988.

Snider, Sarah. "Characteristics of the Part-Time Work Force and Part-Time Employee Participation in Health and Pension Benefits." *Journal of Labor Research* XVI, No. 3 (Summer 1995): 239–248.

About the Authors

LESLIE B. ALEXANDER is Professor of Social Work and Social Research at the Graduate School of Social Work and Social Research at Bryn Mawr College, Bryn Mawr, Pennsylvania. She has made numerous conference presentations and was a visiting research scholar at the Wellesley College Center for Research on Women in 1989–90, where she began work on the current study.

Dr. Alexander has served on the editorial boards of *Social Work* and the *Journal of Social Work Education* and currently serves as a contributing editor of the *American Journal of Orthopsychiatry* and a reviewer for the *Journal of Social Service Research* and *Psychiatric Services*. She is also a member of the Research Committee of the journal *Child and Adolescent Social Work*.

LENARD W. KAYE is Professor of Social Work and Social Research at the Graduate School of Social Work and Social Research at Bryn Mawr College, Bryn Mawr, Pennsylvania. A prolific writer in the field of social gerontology, his recent books include *Controversies in Aging, Home Health Care, New Developments in Home Care Services for the Elderly, Congregate Housing for the Elderly*, and *Men as Caregivers to the Elderly*. Dr. Kaye is on the editorial boards of the *Journal of Gerontological Social Work* and *Geriatric Care Management Journal*, reviews manuscripts for a variety of professional journals, and is a fellow of the Gerontological Society of America.

Acknowledgments

The authors are indebted to numerous individuals who facilitated the successful performance of this research and the publication of its findings.

We are grateful to our editor Carol Buell at Garland Publishing, and to Diana Harris of the University of Tennessee, editor of the Issues in Aging series, for encouraging us to prepare this publication and providing us with important direction for its refinement. We are most appreciative of the generous financial support received from the Families U.S.A. Foundation (formerly the Villers Foundation). The encouragement of Ronald F. Pollak and Cynthia B. Costello at Families U.S.A. is especially noted. Their support represented a pivotal stabilizing force for the researchers. Additional financial support received from the Cassett Foundation, the Faculty Research Fund, and the Madge Miller Fund at Bryn Mawr College, the Emergency Aid of Pennsylvania Foundation, and Wawa, Inc., is also acknowledged with gratitude.

The full cooperation and continuing accessibility of the directors and staff of the four participating senior employment programs must be underscored. Referred to are Marlene Rey at Project Ayuda of the Asociacion Nacional pro Personas Mayores; Peg Gallagher, Janet Francesconi, Ernest Florio, and Edward Reed at the Delaware County Office of Services for the Aging; Aryeh Sherman and Jim Buncy at Seniors at Work of the Jewish Employment and Vocational Service; and Marcia S. Kung, John Carosiello, Marjorie Rooney, and Margaret Gould of the Senior Employment and Education Service.

In addition to contributing a thought-provoking foreword, Professor Hilda Kahne graciously provided helpful suggestions to strengthen the manuscript.

The Bryn Mawr community was instrumental in facilitating the administrative and budgetary execution of the research project, including Dean Ruth W. Mayden, Nona Smith, Diane Craw, and Adrienne D'Amato. Stephen Kauffman deserves special mention for performing all computer programming tasks with great skill and expertise. Many talented graduate students at the school and in the community of social work professionals participated in various phases of the research project, including field interviewing, coding, data entry, and data transcription. Included were Jim Burrill, Liza Clapham, Carey Davis, Terry DeBrule, Alexis Hillman, Sandy Hitschler, Susan Howell, Amy Lehr, Alice McCormick, Sonia Morales, Nayde Perez, Karen Rosenberg, Sherrie K. Schulke, Martha Stephens, Sharon Stern, and Carolyn Wilson. Elizabeth Suarez assumed responsibility for translating the English version of the research protocol into Spanish. We thank Lorraine Wright and Elaine Robertson, who word-processed all study-related documents, including an earlier version of the final report, with patience and precision. We owe a very special thank you to Peg McConnell for performing these same tasks with great expertise and wonderful good humor. Special thanks is also owed to John W. Alexander, Jr., who proofread the entire manuscript and provided invaluable assistance as an editor and caretaker par excellence.

Finally, we are grateful to the many older adults living in the Greater Philadelphia Metropolitan Area who graciously allowed us into their homes and offered us a glimpse into their work lives. They gave unselfishly of their time to respond to what must have seemed like an unending bombardment of questions and inquiries. This analysis was enriched enormously by the breadth of their experiences in America's workplace.

Part-Time Employment for the Low-Income Elderly

Chapter One
Introduction

During the past twenty-five years, there have been increasing demands for the expansion of alternative workplace options including flextime, job-sharing, phased retirement, temporary work, and part-time employment. Of these options, part-time employment has consistently been the most popular and most prevalent (Olmsted and Smith 1994; Olmsted and Trippe 1992; Kahne 1992; and Christensen and Murphree 1988).

While the growth in part-time employment is in part a response to the need for flexibility on the part of dual-worker families and single men and women maintaining young dependents at home (Blank 1990, 1989; Kahne 1994, 1992; Barker 1993; Olmsted and Trippe 1992; and Moen 1994, 1986), there is also evidence of growing interest in part-time work by a range of employers, employment specialists working with the elderly, and the elderly themselves (Bass 1995; Sterns and Sterns 1995; Hirshorn and Hoyer 1994; McNaught and Barth 1992; Louis Harris and Associates 1992; Golden 1992; Kahne 1994, 1992; Sum and Fogg 1990; 9 to 5 1987; Morrison 1986; and National Commission for Employment Policy 1985).

This growing interest in part-time employment for the elderly has been driven by trends both within the older population as well as by the changing landscape of work life in this country. Before considering these changes, we should first indicate how the terms "part-time work" and "older worker" are defined in this study.

Following the U.S. Department of Labor's convention, part-time work is defined as less than 35 hours a week on the job. The term "older worker" is defined as anyone 55 and over, involved in regular paid employment. While there is really no uniform definition of when a worker becomes an older worker (Siegel 1993; Herz 1988; and Irelan, Rabin, and Schwab 1987), with limits as low as age 40 when women are included (Fretz, Gottlich, and Schmoyer 1991), we use 55 and over for two primary reasons. First, some of our study participants were drawn from the Senior Community Service Employment Program, which uses age 55 and above for program eligibility. Furthermore, the Commonwealth Fund's Mature Worker's initiative, also known as The Americans Over 55 at Work Program, used 55 as the lower age limit (Commonwealth Fund 1993).

Trends Within the Older Population

In terms of changes within the older population, there are several relevant trends. First, the numbers of those over 65 grew from 8.1 percent to 12.5 percent of the population between 1950 and 1990 (Kramer 1995). This trend will only become more pronounced as the baby-boom generation ages. According to Barth, McNaught, and Rizzi (1993), by 2020 almost 32 percent of the American population will be 55 and over. To quote:

In actual numbers, this translates into an increase from 51.0 million persons 55 and over in 1990 to more than 93.2 million in 2020. This means that, over the next thirty years, the number of older Americans will grow by 83 percent, while the population age 16 to 54 increases a scant 6 percent. (Barth, McNaught, and Rizzi 1993, 157)

Second, there is ample evidence of increased longevity for both sexes and improved health status for many older Americans. Research has documented the fact that productivity does not tend to decline with age, that older employees are committed to their jobs, that intellectual functioning remains largely constant for most people until they have reached well into later life, and that age alone is a poor indicator of health status (Sterns and Sterns 1995; Sterns and McDaniel 1994; U.S. Department of Health and Human Services 1990; McEvoy and Cascio 1989; Berkowitz 1988; and National Commission on Working Women 1987). For those who work, there is even less of a relationship between aging and health (Kahne 1985). Thus alternative work patterns, such as part-time employment, are being considered with increased seriousness, especially in the context of a rapidly expanding and increasingly active aging population (Bass, Caro, and Chen 1993).

Further, throughout the 1980s and into the 1990s, attitude surveys among older workers and employers continued to document: (1) a strong interest on the part of older employees to continue to work at a reduced schedule beyond retirement, and (2) an acknowledgment by some employers of the positive contributions that older workers could make (Louis Harris and Associates 1992, 1991; American Association of Retired Persons 1989, 1986; Jondrow, Brechling, and Marcus 1987; and 9 to 5 1987).

Although the general view of many employers in the 1960s and 1970s was that worker performance peaked at age 50, surveys of managers in the 1980s revealed more favorable attitudes, both about the performance of older workers and the fact that a larger proportion of older workers would be employed in the future (American Association of Retired Persons 1989; Yankelovich, Skelly, and White 1985; Gollub 1983).

Recent surveys have reported somewhat more ambivalent attitudes on the part of some managers (Peterson and Wendt 1995 and Barth, McNaught, and Rizzi 1995). For example, drawing upon Avolio and Waldman's (1989) meta-analysis of older worker productivity studies, McNaught (1994) concluded that if the relationship between age and productivity was based on impressions of elder co-workers, age was seen as positively influencing productivity. If, on the other hand, managers were asked about the same relationship (between age and productivity), they usually concluded that age negatively influenced worker productivity. In response to the aging of the American population, Barth, McNaught, and Rizzi's (1993) recent conclusion seems well taken:

The workforce within many companies is also graying, but it seems that American businesses have not responded to older workers with the same effort and ingenuity as they have to older customers. (p. 156)

At the same time that the proportion of senior citizens has increased dramatically in recent years—the population aged 55 and over has grown by almost 40 percent in the last two decades—there has also been a striking decrease in the number of older workers in the labor force. As Doeringer (1990b) reported:

In 1967, almost half the population 55 and over spent some time in the labor market. By 1986, this figure had fallen to about one-third, a drop of 25 percent. This reduction in labor market activity has affected all groups of workers, but it has been particularly acute for males and the poorly educated. The decline has also been persistent, even during periods of growth in the demand for labor, and is expected to continue for most segments of the older population to the year 2000 and beyond. A worrisome consequence of these trends is that the balance between those who work and those who do not is tipping. The earnings base of the older population and the opportunities it provides for the accumulation of resources for retirement are shrinking at the same time that life expectancy is increasing. (p. 3)

There have been clear gender differences in the employment of older workers, however. Employment of women has been rising steadily for all age groups. While the proportion of workers who are elderly is small, women make up 43 percent of all workers 55 and over. Further, according to a recent report from the Older Women's League (Kuriansky and Porter forthcoming), while the labor force participation rates for men between the ages of 55 and 64 dropped sharply—from 83 percent in 1970 to 67 percent in 1992—women's participation rates rose slightly—from 43 percent in 1970 to 46.6 percent in 1992. A similar pattern emerged for workers over 65: while men's plummeted, from 26.8 percent in 1970 to 16.2 percent in 1992, women's participation rates dropped slightly, from 9.7 percent in 1970 to 8.3 percent in 1992.

Why has there been such shrinkage in the labor force participation of older adults, especially males? First and foremost has been the increasing trend toward downsizing in many large corporations, resulting in the expansion of early retirement schemes, which are often accompanied by the abrupt departure of older employees, especially older white men, from the workplace.

In fact there is some evidence that older workers are among the demographic groups most threatened by corporate restructuring and downsizing (Useem 1995, 1993). According to a recent report published in *Working Age* ("Alternatives to Downsizing" 1994), 70 percent of American Management Association member companies have downsized since 1988. To quote: "In any one year, one-third to one-half cut their work force by an average of 10 percent. One-fourth have downsized three or more times since 1988" (p. 2). Downsizing has not been limited to the private sector. This same article reported that the Social Security Administration cut its work force by 21 percent between 1985 and 1990.

An additional worrisome trend is early retirement, which has continued in spite of international evidence that has questioned its long-term advisability (Mirkin 1987). There is growing concern that this movement is involuntary for some workers at present, and may become increasingly involuntary in the future (Golden 1992). According to a recent article by Lewis (1994), "More early retirees find the going rough" (p. 1). In this same article, Philip Rones, an economist at the U.S. Department of Labor, concluded that "people who are forced into early retirement by and large are not doing well" (p. 14).

While phased and flexible retirement programs seemed to be taking hold in the early 1980s, and continued to receive worker endorsement, such programs did not continue to expand in the late 1980s. Rather, according to Schrank and Waring (1989): "Despite these many virtues, there are few such programs, and when they are available, there is little participation" (p. 125). Thus in spite of the continued attractiveness of phased retirement schemes on the part of some managers and many workers in the 1990s (Barth, McNaught, and Rizzi (1993), Burkhauser and Quinn's assessment in 1989 still holds: "The modal pattern of retirement still involves an abrupt transition from full-time work to complete labor force withdrawal. Most wage and salary workers who are able to reduce hours must switch jobs to do so" (p. 17).

Additional evidence about widespread worries about retirement came when data was released in 1993 from the first wave of the National Institute on Aging's longitudinal survey. This ongoing survey addresses the retirement of the baby-boom generation and societal aging in general. About 40 percent of the 12,600 respondents, aged 51–60 when first surveyed, reported that they would have no personal income other than Social Security when they retired. Further, over half reported that they felt they could lose their current job within the year. In the event of a layoff, almost half reported that they would have a less than 50–50 chance of getting a new job (National Institute on Aging June 17, 1993). Similar worry was also reported by middle to upper-middle income individuals in a recent *New York Times* article entitled "Retirement's Worried Face" (Uchitelle 1995).

Worry about retirement seems justified for many older Americans. According to Carnevale and Stone (1994):

What many older Americans need is not a spot on the golf course, but a job. Of people 65 and over, 12.2 percent—some 3.6 million—live in poverty. Pension benefits and Social Security are often insufficient to guarantee a decent lifestyle, yet older people continue to be popularly regarded as a leisure class. (p. 102)

Poverty in old age is even more likely if you are a woman, living alone, or an older person of color (National Caucus and Center on Black Aged 1994; Garcia 1993; and Malveaux 1993).

While early-retirement schemes have increased, especially for those in managerial positions, older employees have also been well represented among those workers who were laid off, either because of plant closings or employment cutbacks. For example, between January of 1981 and January of 1986, while about 14 percent of the labor force as a whole left the workplace entirely, more than 33 percent of those workers 55 and over did (Horvath 1987). Between the spans 1977 to 1981 and 1987 to 1993 the permanent-job-loss-unemployment figure increased most dramatically, by 41 percent, for middle-aged workers, those aged 35 to 54. At the same time, however, there was still a 20 percent increase for those 55 and over (Medoff 1993).

Not only are displaced older workers more likely to experience longer spells of unemployment, they are also more likely to withdraw completely from the work force once unemployed (Sicker 1994; Golden 1992; 9 to 5 1987, 1986). Worker discouragement is a very real issue for the older person who has lost a job, and is exacerbated if the worker is a low-income woman or person of color (Malveaux 1993; Sum and Fogg 1990).

Changing Landscape of Work in the United States

Looking more generally at the changing landscape of work in the 1980s and early 1990s, the trend toward downsizing in large corporations, described previously, has been accompanied by a large expansion in the contingent work force. This expansion has been largely a response to the need to become more cost-competitive and flexible in domestic and international markets and to increase quarterly profits (Golden 1992). The result has been the gradual expansion of a number of contingent or conditional work arrangements. These include those of temporary workers; self-employed workers, including consultants, subcontractors, and "life-of-project" workers; business services workers; and some part-time work arrangements. These contingent workers, who lack a strong affiliation and stake with a specific employer, are contrasted with core workers, who do have a strong affiliation and stake with their employer and who represent the more traditional work arrangements which were, until recently, normative in this country (Belous 1989a, 1989b).

Although lacking any official government measure, Belous (1989a) used various data sources to construct an estimate of the size of the contingent work force, which is concentrated largely in services, clerical, and retail trade industries, industries where lower-income older adults are likely to be employed. According to his estimates and those made more recently (Tilly 1996; Parker 1994; and duRivage 1992), nearly one-fourth to one-third of the labor force is now considered contingent workers. This work force is growing at a faster pace than the entire labor force and accounts for a significant number of the jobs created in the 1980s, jobs which may be increasingly filled by older workers in the future.

While these contingent arrangements can reduce labor costs and provide increased flexibility for employers and employees alike, the price of increased flexibility often includes lower wages, fewer fringe benefits, fewer training opportunities, fewer opportunities for advancement, low job security, and unpredictability about working hours (Polivka and Nardone 1989).

Further, as Tilly (1996) has reported:

The new prominence of part-time and temporary jobs brings with it fears of widening instability and insecurity in the work force. . . . If there was a

national fear index, Richard Belous, chief economist for the National Plan-
ning Association, told Time's *reporter, . . . it would be directly related to*
the growth of contingent work. (Castro 1993, 44; in Tilly 1996, 1)

Although there has been increasing attention paid to the aging
worker (see, for example, Bass 1995; Commonwealth Fund 1993;
Doeringer 1990a; and Asbaugh and Fay 1987), and especially those
who work postretirement (see, for example, Herz 1995; Haywood,
Hardy, and Liu 1994; Parnes and Somers 1994; Hardy 1991; and
Myers 1991), there is little empirical research which specifically as-
sesses the actual experience of the older worker in part-time employment. There are a number of questions for which we have no an-
swers. For example, how do race and gender affect the experience of
part-time work? Even though the exploitative potential of part-time
employment is clear, does part-time work prove ultimately advanta-
geous in increasing personal choice for elders? Does the reality of
part-time work mesh with the positive expectations some elders have
about this work option?

There is still not much elder employment research which as-
sesses the experience of low-income female workers and those of
minority backgrounds, who represent the high-growth groups among
the elderly today and are predicted to remain so in the future. These
are also the groups among the elderly who experience the greatest
economic hardships as they age and the greatest vulnerability in the
workplace. According to Doeringer (1990b):

Blacks and Hispanics are two and one-half times more likely to have
these labor market problems (e.g., unemployment, involuntary part-time
work, discouragement from work or low-wage employment) than are
whites, and high school dropouts are twice as likely as college graduates
to be in this category (p. 10). . . . Although no group of older persons is
exempt from employment problems, four groups experience the most se-
vere difficulties—ethnic minorities, women living alone, the working
poor and displaced workers. Unfortunately, these groups are the most
rapidly growing segments of the older population. (p. 8)

Further, according to Doeringer (1990b), at the same time that
retirement is occurring earlier, there is also evidence that "many older

workers take some sort of post-career employment before they retire" (p. 5). What are these "bridge jobs"—jobs following career
employment but preceding retirement (Doeringer 1990b)—like?
What role can part-time jobs play as bridge jobs? On what criteria
should part-time jobs for the elderly be assessed, be they bridge jobs
or otherwise? Can there be such a thing as a "good" part-time job, or
is Levitan and Conway's (1988) bleak characterization of part-timers as "Living on Half-rations" (p. 1) inevitable? How do the low-
income elderly evaluate the part-time jobs that they have—as mostly
"good" or mostly "bad" jobs? How do those low-income workers
who have received jobs through the Senior Community Service
Employment Program regard their jobs?

Since elder part-time workers are a new and emerging group in
the labor force, their special problems have not been a major focus
of conventional manpower and training studies. As a consequence,
whether the wisdom gleaned from such studies applies remains to
be seen. Likewise, as discussed earlier, even though many elders who
have been surveyed in the last fifteen years continue to express a
desire for more part-time work options, we really have very little
empirical data about the actual experience of part-time work for
elders across the social class spectrum. Is there a difference between
the expressed wish for a part-time job, and the reality of the lived
experience of those jobs?

Data on part-time employment is particularly sparse for the low-
income elderly, employed in what have traditionally been characterized as semiskilled and unskilled positions, whose retirement finances
are generally much more precarious than those of many middle-
and upper-middle-class individuals (Calasanti and Bonanno 1992).

Our Study

We used a three-stage research approach, incorporating: (1) an analysis of existing case-record data from workers, 55 years and over, who
were placed in semiskilled and service positions by four job placement and training programs, specializing in the job-seeking needs
of low-income older workers in the Greater Philadelphia region; (2)
intensive in-person and telephone interviews with a random sample
of these older adults; and (3) intensive, open-ended interviews with
key informants from each of the four study sites. Key informants

were asked to elaborate on procedures, problems, and future directions in placing low-income elders in part-time employment.

The following questions helped shape the interpretive framework of the study:

1. What were the expectations about work of low-income older adults seeking or engaging in part-time employment?

2. What kinds of prior work experience had these elders had? How did the part-time jobs that they obtained mesh with their previous work experiences?

3. How did they evaluate their experience with the job-placement agency?

4. What were the structural and functional characteristics of the part-time jobs they obtained?

5. To what extent did these elder workers perceive themselves as exercising some control over their working conditions? If they saw themselves as exercising little control, how much of an issue was this for them?

6. What were the factors contributing to job satisfaction for these low-income elder workers?

7. How did elders evaluate their relationships at work with both same-aged and younger co-workers?

8. Did they report discrimination based on gender, race, national origin, or part-time work status?

9. What was the relationship between gender, race, age, and being a Senior Community Service Employment Program enrollee to the part-time work experience?

10. In terms of overall job quality, were the part-time jobs secured by our respondents mostly "good" or mostly "bad" jobs?

More specifically, chapter 2 presents background data on part-time work for all Americans, including those 55 and over, as well as our interpretive framework. Chapter 3 describes our methodology, followed by a thorough description of our study participants in chapter 4. For the part-time and unemployed participants in our sample, chapter 5 compares their previous work careers, and chapter 6, their experiences with their job-placement programs.

Chapter 7 discusses the structural characteristics, and chapter 8, the functional characteristics of part-time work for our study participants. Chapter 9 presents data on the overall job satisfaction reported by the elder part-time workers, followed in chapter 10 by findings about their levels of perceived discrimination in part-time employment. Chapter 11 presents findings about the attitudes, preferences, and expectations about work and retirement for the part-time elder workers. Chapter 12 discusses the special case of the unemployed elders, and chapter 13, the case of those elders employed full-time in our sample. Finally, based on overall study findings, chapter 14 presents our conclusions and recommendations.

Chapter Two
Part-Time Work
Background and Interpretive Framework

In this chapter we present trends in part-time employment for workers of all ages, followed by data dealing specifically with workers 55 and over. We then briefly review the small body of available empirical research on the elder part-time worker in nongovernmental programs, and existing research on the only government-sponsored training program focused exclusively on securing part-time employment for men and women 55 and over: The Senior Community Service Employment Program (SCSEP).

Next we provide further context for our interpretive framework, including: (1) an understanding of the inherent duality in part-time employment; (2) some of the more disturbing recent trends in the contingent work force, which includes some part-time workers; and (3) some persistent negative stereotypes of part-time work and part-time workers. Drawing upon Friedmann and Havighurst's (1954) definition of the functions of work; conceptions of job quality by Karasek and Theorell (1990), Rosenthal (1989) and Jencks, Perman, and Rainwater (1988); and current perspectives about the characteristics of "good" and "bad" part-time work by Tilly (1996, 1992b), Kahne (1994, 1992, and 1985), and Blank (1997, 1990), we close this chapter by posing the criteria we will use—our interpretive framework—to assess whether the part-time positions obtained by the elders in our study were mostly "good" or mostly "bad" part-time jobs.

Part-Time Employment: All Workers
Unlike other alternative work schedules, part-time employment, defined as less than 35 hours a week by the U.S. Department of Labor, has literally exploded in the last 24 years. Between 1969 and

1993, the numbers of all employed persons working part-time increased from 10.8 million to 20.7 million, representing a 91.7 percent increase during this period. Although part-time work increased 91.7 percent, it is important to keep in mind that its growth as a percentage of the total work force during those same years was minimal—from 15.5 percent in 1969 to 18.8 percent in 1993 (Saltford and Snider 1994, 1). Therefore, over four-fifths of all Americans who work continue to do so full-time.

Who are these part-time employees? Based on 1993 figures from the Current Population Survey, Saltford and Snider (1994) reported:

Part-time work is a major form of employment for three demographic groups in our society: younger workers (aged 16–17), older workers (aged 65 and over), and female workers. In 1992, the majority of people aged 16–17 (56 percent) and 65 and older (85 percent) were not in the labor force. However, of the 2.9 million workers aged 16–17 who were employed in 1992, 84.4 percent were part-time. Of the 4.6 million workers aged 65 and older who were employed, 56.3 percent were part-time. By contrast, 13.4 percent of workers aged 45–54 and 14.6 percent of those aged 25–44 were part-time. (p. 15)

In 1993, the gender distribution for *all* part-time workers over the age of 16 was 65 percent female and 35 percent male. If all part-time workers were considered, there were few differences between the percentages of females and males working part-time in two age groups: those between the ages of 16 to 24, and those 45 and over. As expected, there were more pronounced gender differences for those between the ages of 25 and 44. Twenty-six percent of all part-time workers were females aged 25 to 44; nine percent of all part-time workers were males aged 25 to 44 (Saltford and Snider 1994, 17).

Given these figures, Saltford and Snider's conclusion is well taken:

. . . part-time work, for many, is part of a work life cycle, with individuals working part-time when they are younger, then moving into full-time positions throughout their prime working years and, finally, as retirement nears, returning to part-time employment. (p. 15)

In 1993, all part-timers worked an average of 21.7 hours per week (Blank 1997, Table 1). Drawing on 1993 Current Population Survey data, but this time unpublished figures, Saltford and Snider (1994) reported that the median hourly wage for all part-time workers was $5.55, or 62 percent of the median hourly wage of $8.89 for full-time workers. Note that this ratio between part- and full-time workers' hourly earnings has changed very little since 1973 (Saltford and Snider 1994, 17).

When these same income figures for 1993 were compared by gender, the results were: for men, the part-time hourly wage of $5.19 was 52 percent of the median hourly wage of $9.89 for men working full-time; for women, the median hourly wage of $5.75 for all part-time workers was 72 percent of the median hourly wage of $7.94 for women working full-time (Saltford and Snider 1994, 17).

In terms of family type, in 1992 almost one-half (46.1 percent) of all part-time workers were married. While about 13.3 percent of all married male workers were employed part-time, almost a third of all married females worked part-time. This figure increased to almost 40 percent for married women with children, but decreased to about 10 percent for married men with children (Saltford and Snider 1994, 18).

In terms of race and national origin, in 1992 about 22 percent of whites indicated they worked part-time compared to about 19 percent each for African Americans and Hispanics. However, somewhat larger percentages of African Americans (7.2 percent) and Hispanics (7.9 percent) reported working part-time *involuntarily* than whites (4.6 percent).

In 1992, 60 percent of all part-time workers were concentrated in retail trade (41 percent) and services (29 percent). Further, slightly over half of all part-time workers were working in small firms (e.g., those with fewer than 100 employees); 32 percent were in firms with fewer than 10 employees. In 1993, only about 8 percent of part-timers were represented by unions (Saltford and Snider 1994, 13–14).

From this review of recent data on all Americans who work part-time, it is clear that part-time workers are a heterogeneous group. Further, each major group of part-timers—younger workers; women, typically those with children at home; and workers over 65—can have a somewhat different set of reasons for desiring the flexibility afforded by part-time employment, a point we will address further subsequently.

Part-Time Work: Those 55 and Over

For those 55 and over, the incidence of part-time work increases with age. In 1984, approximately 32 percent of those 55 and over were in the labor force, with one-quarter working part-time. While only 13 percent of those *65 and older* were in the labor force, almost one-half were working part-time, which was over twice the rate for all workers (9 to 5 1986). In 1990, 3.8 million people over *age 55*, or about 25 percent of those over 55 who worked, worked part-time. Of these, 41 percent were men and 59 percent were women. Almost 90 percent were white (Christensen et al. 1992, 44).

Even though the total labor-force participation rate of those 65 and over has been shrinking, part-time employment is holding steady and has in fact increased considerably since 1969. In 1969 those 65 and older working part-time represented 41 percent of all in that age group who were employed. By 1979, this figure had risen to 52 percent, where it held steady through 1988 (Tilly 1992b). As we report subsequently, there is recent evidence suggesting that this trend of expanding part-time employment for workers 65 and over is continuing in the 1990s and may even be increasing somewhat.

According to Christensen, Axel, Hewitt, and Nardone (1992), older contingent workers can be divided into three distinct categories. The first consists of retirees, who generally have a pension, health benefits in many cases, and possibly some savings. They are typically either self-employed or working part-time because they don't want to stop working entirely or they want to supplement their retirement income. While exact figures were not provided, this is undoubtedly the smallest group of older contingent workers—one that also includes the smallest number of older women and persons of color.

The second group includes middle managers, forced out of their jobs because of downsizing, who are typically male, white collar, and well-educated. This group is forced into part-time employment because they cannot find regular full-time work.

The third group are chronic contingent workers, primarily women and minorities of both genders, with limited safety nets, who have spent a lifetime in semiskilled and unskilled jobs, primarily in retail sales or the service sector. The majority of our respondents fell into this group. Further, just as the three major groups of all part-time workers—the young, women with children, and the elderly—are heterogeneous in terms of why they work part-time, the three major groups of elder part-time workers, identified above, are heterogeneous as well.

It is amply clear that the "pin money" image of part-time work is not applicable for the vast majority of all part-time employees, but especially for the third group of elder part-timers, identified above. As Warme, Lundy, and Lundy (1992) concluded for all part-time workers:

. . . the "mad money" image of part-time work is untenable today, laid to rest by the increase in the working poor, the expanding numbers of involuntary part-time workers, the growth of single-parent families, the insufficiency of family incomes, the failure of Social Security to provide adequately for those with disabilities, and the increasing economic vulnerability of women at all stages of their lives. (p. 3)

Other Empirical Research on Elder Part-Time Workers

In the early 1980s, the few researchers who used experimental approaches to examine part-time work for the elderly reported generally favorable responses to this work pattern, particularly in terms of positive effects on measures of perceived health, life satisfaction, and job satisfaction (see, for example, Soumerai and Avorn 1983 and Shapiro and Roos 1982).

As part of the Commonwealth Fund's Americans Over 55 at Work Program, an evaluation was done in the fall of 1990 and the spring of 1991 of the elder workers' initiatives of two American companies—Days Inns of America and the Traveler's Insurance Company, and one British company, B&Q. We will focus on the results from the two American companies. Beginning in the early 1980s, the Traveler's Insurance Company began using some of their own retirees as part-time staff to service their customer-service hotline. This program has expanded and has been evaluated as good for the retirees and cost-effective for the company. While only about one-third of the older workers worked part-time, Days Inns' experience with older workers as reservations clerks was positive for workers and employer alike (Commonwealth Fund 1991).

Based on their national survey in late 1991 and early 1992, Hirshorn and Hoyer (1994) reported basically optimistic findings about the hiring and utilization of retirees by private firms with 20 or more employees. They found that: (1) over 46 percent of private-sector firms hired retirees, including those who had previously worked for the firm and those who had not; (2) over 60 percent of both the part- and full-time retirees worked year-round; (3) about 52 percent worked part-time; (4) retirees worked in a range of occupational placements; and (5) there were relatively few numbers of retirees in any one firm. At the same time, however, the hiring of retirees was largely an informal practice. Less than 10 percent of the firms interviewed had any written policy regarding the hiring of retirees.

While not all specific to part-time work alone and limited to males, there is recent evidence, drawn from large-scale data sets, indicating that some early retirees are returning to work in larger numbers than formerly believed. For example, Herz (1995), using data from March 1985, 1989, and 1993 Current Population Surveys, found that both full- and part-time work among retired men younger than 65 had increased markedly, a fact not reflected in overall labor-force participation rates.

Using data from the National Longitudinal Survey of Older Men, Haywood, Hardy, and Liu (1994) found that re-entry occurred quickly, typically within the first year or two after retirement. For the almost one-third of retirees who returned to work, about a third of them returned part-time. Using this same data set, Parnes and Summers (1994) examined the work experiences of a cohort of men born between 1906 and 1921, who were in their 70s and 80s when interviewed in late 1990. More than one in six were employed when interviewed; about two-thirds worked part-time. Among the characteristics most determinant of the continued employment of these men long after conventional retirement were good health, a distaste for retirement, and a strong commitment to work.

Further, Anderson, Burkhauser, and Slotsve (1992), using data from the Panel Study of Income Dynamics, compared the work and retirement decisions of males who retired in the 1970s with those who retired in the 1980s. They discovered that work after retire-

ment was a common event, one that occurred more quickly following retirement in the 1980s than in the 1970s. According to their
data, these postretirement jobs were more likely to be part-time.

As mentioned above, these studies just described are recent and
are all limited to the experiences of men. There is little in-depth
empirical data specifically assessing the experience of part-time work
for that third group of older workers, described by Christensen, Axel,
Hewitt, and Nardone (1992)—those male, female, and minority
workers who have spent the majority of their work lives in semiskilled and unskilled work, largely in the retail sales and service sectors, as was true for the majority of the participants in our study.

While there are indications that many older workers, especially
those 65 and over, actually prefer part-time employment, other disturbing evidence, reviewed in chapter 1, suggests that some elderly
may be forced into these jobs because of family responsibilities, ill-
ness, disability, the impact of federal retirement laws, forced early
retirement, and the unavailability of full-time work (Sicker 1994;
Doeringer 1990a; 9 to 5 1987; Robinson, Coberly, and Paul 1985).
According to Sum and Fogg (1990), approximately 36 percent of
the increase in part-time employment among older persons between
March 1974 and March 1987 occurred for economic reasons. It has
been further suggested that those older workers who work part-time
involuntarily are placed in the exploited position of serving as the
"shock absorbers" for a changing American economy (9 to 5 1987,
iii).

Research on Government-sponsored Training Programs for the Elderly: The Senior Community Service Employment Program (SCSEP)

Before briefly reviewing the SCSEP research, it should be noted that
most federal training money has not been spent for older workers,
but rather has been geared primarily to workers between the ages of
25 and 44 (Rix 1990). Of the government-sponsored training programs for the elderly today, there are two primary ones. The first
includes programs financed under the Job Training Partnership Act
(JTPA) and the second, the Senior Community Service Employment Program (SCSEP), funded through Title V of the Older Americans Act. We will limit our review to SCSEP for two reasons. First,

this is the only government-sponsored program geared specifically to placing workers 55 and over in part-time positions. Only 3 percent of funds under JTPA are targeted specifically to this same-aged population (Barth, McNaught, and Rizzi 1993, 65). And second, about one-half of our study respondents were enrolled in SCSEP programs. Formal research on SCSEP programs, which have maintained very low visibility since their inception, has been rare (Freedman 1994).

In the mid-1980s, Centaur Associates (1986) and the National Caucus and Center on Black Aged, Inc. (1987), performed program evaluations of selected SCSEP programs across the country. Mathematica Policy Research Institute, Inc., performed an additional evaluation in 1994 of the 502(e) programs (Allin and Decker 1994). These are experimental programs, designed to place older adults in unsubsidized employment in the private sector. These 502(e) programs are authorized by SCSEP legislation and operated by the local SCSEP sites, which can use a portion of their SCSEP allotment to sponsor them. These 502(e) programs can include both SCSEP and non-SCSEP enrollees, can pay more than the federal minimum wage, and can subsidize a greater number of hours a week than SCSEP programs, which are limited to 20 hours.

As part of the Commonwealth Fund's Americans Over 55 at Work Program, Freedman (1994) interviewed selective SCSEP personnel and program participants nationwide as part of a larger exploration of the potential for expanding senior service opportunities in this country. Finally, the Department of Labor sponsored two recent, small research projects: (1) a survey of 152 SCSEP administrators (Cox 1995) and (2) an in-depth interview study of 30 enrollees and 22 family members from a Colorado SCSEP program (Dooley 1995).

While further programmatic details about the SCSEP program are provided in chapter 3, the general consensus resulting from the small body of formal research performed on this program is as follows. On the downside, it serves a very small percentage of the eligibles in any one year and in fact has never served more than about 65,000 to 70,000 elders nationwide (Freedman 1994; Sandell 1988). Low appropriations have been a consistent problem for this program. Further, some have argued that it provides the same bridge jobs which are already available to older workers; has not successfully reached the hardest to serve groups including Hispanics, Asians, and the working poor; and has rarely included a training component—one which would facilitate the movement of elders from subsidized to unsubsidized employment (Doeringer 1990b). It is also a program whose current funding levels are severely threatened (Kilborn 1995).

On the positive side, however, evaluative efforts mentioned above have consistently reported high degrees of satisfaction on the part of enrollees, who have regularly indicated that the program has provided needed income and meaningful work, and has overall made a positive impact on their lives. As Kilborn recently reported about SCSEP programs in general:

A small piece of the Great Society provides work, wages, and hope. . . . Further, according to one program director in rural Georgia: There are vast numbers of older people who are one major problem from the poor house. . . . The furnace blows up. The car quits. The roof needs to be repaired. The spouse dies, or gets sick. And some, he said, are not ready to work. . . . They need glasses, or clothes or shoes or teeth, he said, so Green Thumb (one of the national non-profit sponsors of SCSEP programs) helps out. (Kilborn 1995, A16)

Part-Time Work for Elders: The Optimistic View

Until the mid-1980s, there was considerable enthusiasm about the expansion of part-time employment for elders. As reviewed in chapter 1, there is ample evidence about the increased longevity of both sexes, their improved health status, and the fact that intellectual functioning remains largely constant for most people well into old age.

Until the mid-1980s, part-time work for elders was seen as a way: (1) to ease the transition into retirement—the so-called bridging function (Doeringer 1990a); (2) to provide supplemental income; and (3) to offer the opportunity for an additional career for some elders (Commonwealth Fund 1987). The flexibility that part-time work could afford was viewed as highly desirable. The small quantity of existing research about part-time work for the elderly also reported generally favorable responses to this work pattern, especially in terms of the positive effects on measures of perceived health, life satisfaction, and job satisfaction (Soumerai and Avorn 1983; Shapiro and Roos 1982).

As mentioned in chapter 1, there has also been consistent evidence that many older workers express preferences for continuing to work, and for working part-time. Further, as reported in the 1992 Louis Harris and Associates Survey of 2,999 noninstitutionalized persons 55 and over, about one-third of both men and women working full-time said they would prefer to work part-time, suggesting a disparity between the preferences of older people and the realities of the workplace (Barth, McNaught, and Rizzi 1995, 44).

Part-Time Work: The Inherent Duality

There has long been a recognition of the inherent duality in part-time work. Kahne was one of the first to acknowledge this characteristic, introducing the notions of New Concept and Old Concept part-time work in her 1985 book, *Reconceiving Part-Time Work*. This book specifically addressed part-time employment for older workers and for women. At that time, she found numerous examples in both the public and private sectors of New Concept part-time work. New Concept part-time work was characterized by secure job attachment; career potential, including opportunities for ongoing job training; and wages and benefits prorated to those of equivalent full-time workers.

On the other hand, Old Concept part-time work, which has always been more prevalent, was characterized by low wages, few or no fringe benefits, low productivity, insecure job attachment and high turnover, with little or no opportunity for career advancement or additional training. (Kahne 1985, 75)

Somewhat later, Tilly (1996, 1992a, and 1992b) made the distinction between retention or "good" part-time work (akin to New Concept part-time work) and secondary or "bad" part-time work (akin to Old Concept part-time work). Secondary part-time work is characterized by low pay, few fringe benefits, low skill, low productivity, and high turnover. To quote:

Secondary part-time employment thus represents one form of what labor market economists call a secondary *labor market—a set of jobs charac-*

terized by high turnover and little opportunity for advancement. (Tilly 1992b, 20)

On the other hand, retention part-time jobs are those created to attract or retain valued workers whose life circumstances prevent them from working full-time. To quote:

Retention part-time work arrangements tend to be offered only to workers in relatively skilled jobs. Unlike secondary part-time employment, retention part-time work is characterized by high compensation, high productivity, and low turnover—all features of what labor economists call a primary labor market. In these jobs, managers accommodate worker preferences as compared to secondary part-time employment where workers seldom have a choice." (Tilly 1992b, 20)

Based on his analysis of the retail and insurance industries, a high part-time and low part-time sector, respectively, Tilly indicated that "good" part-time jobs, such as those held by professional and technical workers, were good because they were located within a primary labor market; "bad" part-time jobs, such as those held by retail clerks and insurance clerks were bad because they were located within a secondary labor market.

In his view, then, part-time work is not inherently good or bad, but assumes its character depending on the particular internal labor market within which it is located. The upside is that there can be potentially "good" part-time employment. The downside is that almost two-thirds of all part-time work today is located within a secondary labor market—in the lower-paid retail sales and services industries—which are anticipated to expand further in the future and where most part-time elder workers are employed (Tilly 1996, 1992a; Saltford and Snider 1994; and duRivage 1992).

Part-Time and Other Contingent Work: The Downside for Elders and Others

Even though there was still some optimism by the mid-1980s that New Concept work was increasing (Kahne 1985), since the late 1980s, the predominantly positive view about part-time employment has been continually challenged. There are several components to this challenge, including: (1) the expansion of *involuntary* part-time work; (2) the expansion of other contingent work arrangements and their potential negative consequences; and (3) the persistent negative stereotypes about part-time work and workers.

a. Involuntary Part-Time Work: For All Workers and Those 55 and Older

First and foremost has been the increasing, and according to some economists, alarming growth in involuntary part-time work (Tilly 1996, 1992a and 1992b; Appelbaum 1992a and 1992b; and Callaghan and Hartmann 1991). Tilly (1992b) and Callaghan and Hartmann (1991) reported that almost all of the growth of part-time employment since 1970 was involuntary—in other words, individuals working part-time who would prefer full-time hours. Between 1970 and 1990, "involuntary part-time employment more than doubled (grew 121 percent) while voluntary part-time employment as well as total employment (full- and part-time) grew by 57 and 54 percent respectively" (Callaghan and Hartmann 1991, 4). Since 1976, there was also evidence that the hours part-time workers worked were also growing faster than those of full-time workers (Callaghan and Hartmann 1991). This growth of involuntary part-time work continues to be experienced disproportionately by women, teens, and black workers—those who already experience discrimination in employment. Even though reporting strategies impeded their exact count until very recently, there was also evidence of growth in multiple part-time job holders (Tilly 1992a).

In 1988, of the roughly 18.4 percent of all workers working part-time, approximately 4.7 percent were working part-time *involuntarily*. Looking at women first, of those who were single (never married or no longer married), 6.5 percent were working part-time involuntarily. For workers over 65, the percentage was somewhat less—4.5 percent. While women were more likely to choose part-time work, they were also more likely to be stuck in part-time jobs against their will. The female rate of involuntary part-time work was 44 percent greater than for men (Tilly 1992a, 1992b).

What about figures specific to older workers, employed part-time *involuntarily?* As mentioned previously, these figures are somewhat less accessible, since the alarm about involuntary part-time work has been sounded more for younger workers with families. As mentioned above, Tilly reported that in 1988, 4.5 percent of those *65 and older* were working part-time involuntarily. Kuriansky and Porter (forthcoming) reported that in 1991, 5.5 percent of female workers 55 and older were working part-time involuntarily, compared to 3.8 percent of same-aged men (p. 6). These figures were fairly comparable to those of younger men and women. Christensen, Axel, Hewitt, and Nardone concluded in 1992 that the majority of part-time workers 55 and older worked part-time voluntarily and that voluntary part-time work increased with age (p. 44).

How problematic is this expansion in involuntary part-time work for workers of all ages? There are mixed opinions about the interpretation of this increase and its consequences. Tilly (1996), who is quite alarmed about this expansion, pointed out that for those employed in this fashion:

An involuntary part-time job is only half a job in the sense that it is only half the job that the employee wants. . . . At the same time, millions of full-time workers would prefer part-time hours but are unable to obtain them, while millions of others remain jobless as they search for a part-time job.

Throughout 1993, an average of 6.1 million Americans, or 5.5 percent of those at work, were working part-time involuntarily—a number comparable to the annual average of 6.5 million who were unemployed (U.S. Bureau of Labor Statistics, Employment and Earnings, January 1994, p. 4). (p. 3)

Kahne has also expressed more concern recently about the likelihood of further expansion of New Concept part-time work, which is, by definition, voluntarily chosen. For example, her article in the 1992 Warme, Lundy, and Lundy volume was entitled: "Part-Time Work: A Hope and a Peril." In her most recent article (1994), she pointed out that part-time work has always been controversial. At the same time that it has provided the flexibility and the opportunity to maintain continuous work force attachment for families with children, some of this expansion in part-time work has also been a way for businesses to cut costs and has been viewed by some as a threat to the work standards and wage levels of full-time workers (Kahne 1994, 417). She further acknowledged that

. . . although the numbers of voluntary part-time workers are increasing with the growth of the labor force, so too are the numbers of involuntary part-timers. Between 1972 and 1992, this proportion grew from 16 to 24 percent among women part-time workers and from 33 to 40 percent among men who were part-timers. (p. 418)

Saltford and Snider (1994) take a somewhat different tack. While acknowledging that the number of persons working part-time involuntarily increased from 4.5 percent of all workers (4.9 million) to 5.5 percent of all workers (6.1 million workers) between 1990 and 1993, they further reported that the levels of involuntary part-time workers were actually greater in 1982–83, following the recession in the early 1980s (6.5 percent of total workers in both years), than in the 1990s (p. 11).

Further, Blank (1997) pointed out the disparities between men and women in involuntary part-time work. She reported that during the past twenty-five years, between 26 percent and 30 percent of the entire female labor force has consistently worked part-time. Of this group, about 15 percent reported working part-time involuntarily in 1970, while about 25 percent reported working involuntarily in 1993. While the percentage of all men working part-time increased about 4 percentage points between 1970 and 1993 (from 8.4 percent to 12.8 percent), the percentage working part-time involuntarily grew from 25 percent in 1970 to about 33 percent in 1993. Even so, Blank argues that the case should not be overstated, since the vast majority of *both* male and female workers working part-time have indicated that they were seeking only part-time work and were doing so voluntarily (pp. 10–11).

b. A Note of Explanation about Contingent Work and Its Expansion in the 1990s

Not only has part-time employment mushroomed, but there has also been expansion in other areas of the contingent work force, which we now review. As mentioned in chapter 1, for some economists (see, for example, Tilly 1996, 1992a and 1992b; Appelbaum 1992a and 1992b; duRivage 1992; and Callaghan and Hartmann 1991), the expansion of the contingent work force is alarming because it represents a widening insecurity and instability in the work force, which may reflect a continuing and more permanent change in the overall makeup of the labor force in this country.

While we briefly referred to the definition of contingent work as conditional work in chapter 1, we should further clarify the meaning of this term. Originally coined by economist Audrey Freedman at a 1985 conference on employment security, contingent work is now identified with a wide range of work arrangements (Polivka and Nardone 1989), including many part-time and temporary workers; on-call workers; self-employed workers, including consultants, subcontractors, and "life-of-project" workers; and business service workers. These contingent or ring workers, lacking a strong affiliation and stake with a specific employer, are contrasted with core workers who do have a strong affiliation and stake with their employer. These core workers represented the more traditional work arrangements which were normative in this country until recently (Belous 1989a and 1989b). In other words, contingent workers are defined by the status of their job—"those who are employed in jobs that don't fit the traditional description of a full-time permanent job with benefits" (Callaghan and Hartmann 1991, 1).

Polivka and Nardone expressed concern in 1989 about the broadness of the definition of contingency, arguing that it was misleading to define contingent jobs primarily on the basis of their permanency. For example, in the case of part-time employment,

... *many part-time workers are as attached to their jobs as full-time workers. . . . In January of 1987, half of all part-time workers ages 25 and older had 3.9 years or more of tenure with their current employers. This is about 80 percent of the median tenure of full-time workers. (p. 10)*

They went on to urge that the term "contingency" be based more narrowly on the terms of employment. For them, the most important characteristic of contingent work was a *lack of job security*, which included not only jobs of short duration, but also jobs whose future continuation was uncertain. They provided the example of a substitute teacher, who took the place of a teacher on maternity leave. Even though the actual duration of the job could be a year or more, the essential issue defining the contingency of this position was the fact that there was no expectation of future employment.

Further, for Polivka and Nardone (1989), the second most important characteristic of contingent work was not the number of hours worked but whether these hours could be changed *unpredictably* by either employer, or for that matter, employee. For them, the provision of benefits was less of an issue in its own right, but one best viewed as dependent on the long-term nature of the relationship.

Put another way and expanded a bit recently, Saltford and Snider (1994) stated:

Contingency work implies shifts in three traditional notions of employment: time—something different from an 8-hour, 5-day week; permanency—something other than a permanent relationship between employer and employee; and social contract—something different from the traditional reciprocal rights, protections, and obligations between the worker and the employer (Christensen and Murphree 1988). Employers often use contingent workers to surround a core of full-time workers. (p. 7)

It is important to note here that even today, not all part-time work can be classified as contingent work, as exemplified by Tilly's description of retention part-time work and Kahne's New Concept part-time work. Also, contingency can best be thought of as a variable quality of overall work practices rather than a dichotomous characteristic. In other words, there can be degrees of contingency in a work arrangement, rather than an all-or-nothing characterization.

Returning to broader trends in the expansion of the contingent labor force, particularly explosive growth has occurred in the temporary-help industry, which expanded ten times as fast as overall employment between 1982 and the recession onset in 1990 (Appelbaum 1992a and 1992b). According to Fierman (1994):

Manpower, the biggest of the 7,000 U.S. temp agencies, is now also the nation's biggest private employer, with roughly 600,000 people on its payroll. That's some 200,000 more employees than General Motors and 345,000 more than IBM. (p. 31)

Golden (1992) has estimated that about 10 percent of those 55 and over are hired through temporary help services.

A final area of contingent growth, which is even harder to count, are workers employed off-the-books. Christensen (1990) reported that for most of the elders she interviewed, motivations were varied:

. . . most saw nothing morally or legally wrong in working off the books and not paying taxes. For them it was a practical decision [p. 191]. . . . As long as the jobs that are available to older workers tend to be of a low-skilled or low-paying nature, we can expect many older Americans to do them off the books. But even if the job quality is enhanced, there will probably always be some workers who want to earn that extra little amount and not report it. (p. 194)

c. Other Negative Consequences of Increasing Part-Time and Contingent Work

As presented by Tilly (1992a and 1992b) and duRivage (1992), and still applicable today, the following are some of the obvious perils of much part-time and other forms of contingent work.

Average part-time workers typically earn only 60 percent of the median hourly wage of full-time workers. Less than 25 percent have any employer-sponsored health-insurance coverage. Most are barred from other fringe benefits as well.

One in six part-time workers and one in five involuntary part-timers has an income below the poverty level, compared to one in 37 of full-time workers.

Eighty-nine percent of part-time and contingent workers, compared to 54 percent of current full-time workers, lack pension coverage.

Most contingent work falls outside of the net of worker protection, such as ERISA, unemployment insurance, and COBRA. Likewise, part-time and contingent workers get fewer Social Security credits in general. In addition, unions face large obstacles in bargaining for part-time and contingent workers.

Part-time and contingent workers typically have little access to career paths, seniority, and job training opportunities. According to Carre (1992), while such positions often provide the mechanisms for elders to enter or reenter the work force, "as points of entry, however, these jobs often are not connected to the rest of the employment structure within a firm. Thus by entering the labor market through these jobs, women may find their options for future advancement limited" (p. 75). Further, according to Olmsted (1985), contingent workers rarely even have a performance review.

d. Why the Expansion in Contingent Work?

What has fueled this expansion? According to Tilly (1992a and 1992b), Carre (1992), and Appelbaum (1992a and 1992b), this expansion is not due primarily to demographic shifts or to accommodate worker preferences for flexibility, but rather is more a response to employers' need to respond to changes in technology and increased international competition by shifting the risks of economic uncertainty onto workers.

Christensen, Axel, Hewitt, and Nardone (1992) interpreted the growth in contingent arrangements for older workers as an overall lack of concern for this group of workers. For these authors, this lack of concern was confirmed by a follow-up survey by Towers Perrin, which indicated that only

14 percent of companies are developing any strategies to deal with an older workforce. Sixty percent said that they were simply not concerned, and on a recent Conference Board Survey, CEOs ranked concern about the aging workforce fourteenth out of sixteen issues. (Christensen, Axel, Hewitt, and Nardone 1992, 42)

Callaghan and Hartmann (1991) reported a similar attitudinal bias toward all contingent workers, saying that

in general it would be useful for employers to keep in mind that little about work arrangements is technologically determined. Much is determined by custom and tradition that in this period of economic transition for the United States should be carefully scrutinized. (p. 32)

The Persistence of Negative Stereotypes of Part-Time Work and Workers

Currently, there are several nonprofit organizations, including Catalyst, New Ways to Work, 9 to 5, and the Association of Part-Time Professionals, devoted to providing information and training on various work-time options, part-time work included. In spite of their and others' efforts to promote a new concept of part-time work, including conditions of permanent employment, with career potential, as well as wages and benefits prorated to those of equivalent full-time workers, both the myths and realities of much part-time work remain rather negative. Most part-time work is not usually considered, and often is not, in reality, very desirable work with respect to pay, benefits, prestige, promotional opportunity, intrinsic rewards, and the probability of developing stable, supportive relationships with co-workers and supervisors (see, for example, Tilly 1996, 1992a, and 1992b; Appelbaum 1992a and 1992b; duRivage 1992; and Callaghan and Hartmann 1991). As Meister stated directly in 1988, which still characterizes the overall societal attitude toward part-time employees today: "Part timers are second-class workers" (p. 21-A).

Just as negative stereotypes and ambivalence persist about the employability of the elderly in terms of their skills, capacities, and potential, the same holds true for part-time work. In 1985, Barney Olmsted, former co-director of New Ways to Work, a nonprofit organization that focuses on flexible workplace hours for men and women, summed up the prevailing attitudes toward and reality of much part-time work then, which are also still applicable today:

Another problem is the widely held belief that part-time workers are less motivated, dependable and productive than full-timers. Although there are considerable data that have refuted this bias, it is still widely held and is a primary reason for the limited number of good part-time jobs that are available, particularly in higher-level classifications. (p. 4)

Some evidence suggests that elders who work part-time may be in double jeopardy. Although this was stated by Soumerai and Avorn in 1983, we will examine its continuing applicability today in our study:

First, older people are prime candidates for salary exploitation, since as workers they are in great supply at a time of slight demand and restrictions of Social Security currently prevent their openly receiving more than small sums. . . . Other programs attempting to tap the res-

ervoir of retiree labor run the risk of replacing forced inactivity in the old with indentured labor. . . . Further, in a faltering economy, temptation will be great to displace currently employed workers with part-time elderly quasi-volunteers, reversing the usual order of age bias. No matter how cost containing, such a strategy could intensify inter-generational economic right. Although the opportunity *to work far into advanced age may be a right owed to every citizen, such a right could easily be distorted into an obligation at a time when publicly supported pension systems are under increasing economic pressure. (pp. 361–62)*

Having extensively reviewed the changing context and evaluation of part-time work over the last ten years, we now present our interpretive framework, which draws upon the following: (1) the functions of part-time work for the elderly; (2) definitions of job quality; and (3) current perspectives about the characteristics of "good" and "bad" part-time work. Drawing upon these three perspectives, we end this chapter by presenting the criteria we will use to assess whether the part-time jobs obtained by our study respondents were mostly "good" or mostly "bad" part-time jobs.

Major Functions of Part-Time Work for the Elderly

As indicated above, part-time workers today are a rather heterogeneous group, consisting of working mothers, teens, and elder workers, each with a rather different set of reasons for working part-time. Further, as indicated by Christensen, Axel, Hewitt, and Nardone (1992), there is also heterogeneity among workers 55 and over in terms of why they work part-time and their subsequent experience of part-time employment. Our research is concerned specifically with the functions part-time work serves for the low-income elderly, many of whom are women and minorities.

In their pioneering work on the functions of full-time work for employees, Friedmann and Havighurst (1954) identified the following five: (1) *income or financial return;* (2) work as *a regulator* of life-activity, which gives order and routine to a worker's life; (3) work as a *provider of a sense of identity,* which is critical both to the individual and to his/her standing in the community; (4) work as a basis for *important social relationships*, both in terms of social contact and as a major reference group; and (5) work as the *provider of meaning-ful life experiences.* To what extent these same functions hold true for low-income part-time elder workers remains unknown and is inves-tigated further in our study.

Job Quality

While wage levels used to be the primary indicator of job quality (Rosenthal, 1989), discussions of this topic—especially those of Karasek and Theorell (1990); Rosenthal (1989); Jencks, Perman, and Rainwater (1988)—indicate that increasingly, *nonwage* aspects of jobs are being considered as equal to, or even more important in some cases than, wages alone in the evaluation of overall job quality. Although the constellation of nonwage characteristics varied some-what for each author, there was, at the same time, considerable over-lap. For Rosenthal (1989) there were five major sets of variables which were critical to the assessment of job quality: (1) *job duties* and *work-ing conditions*, including such things as whether the job was hazard-ous, repetitious, required physical stamina, involved working with detail, involved working as part of a team, was located in a confined work space, involved stress, and the extent to which there was worker autonomy; (2) *job satisfaction*, including such things as the opportu-nity to use existing skills, acquire new skills, and the opportunity to problem-solve and exercise creativity; (3) *the period of work,* whether weekend or shift, overtime, or involving flexible work hours; (4) *job security,* and (5) the degree of *social status* involved with the job.

Jencks, Perman, and Rainwater (1988) provided thirteen nonmonetary criteria in addition to wages, which characterized a good job. In addition to qualities having to do with repetitious work, job security, on-the-job training, and flexible working hours, these authors added the following characteristics: the hours spent at work, the number of paid vacation days, education requirements, getting dirty at work, frequent supervision, whether your own boss had a boss, whether there was a union contract at the job-site, and whether or not the worker was a state/local or federal employee. While they concluded that earnings were still the most important single indica-tor of a job's desirability, "the 13 non-monetary job characteristics together are twice as important as earnings. Unlike occupational status and earnings, the proposed index (IJD, or index of job desirability) explains almost the entire effect of race, sex, educational, attainment, and experience on job ratings" (p. 1322).

Finally, Karasek and Theorell (1990), in their book *Healthy Work*, broke down job quality into six major psychosocial work dimensions. These included: (1) *decision latitude,* or the amount of skill, discretion, and individual authority and autonomy workers had; (2) *psychological job demands,* including not having to work too hard, too fast, too excessively, or in the context of conflicting demands; (3) *job insecurity,* or the degree to which the position was not steady, had poor job security, and involved a high likelihood of lay-offs; (4) *the extent of hazardous exposure;* (5) the *degree of physical exertion;* and (6) the amount of *social support* provided, both by supervisors and co-workers.

While neither of the formal assessment instruments evolving from Jencks, Perman, and Rainwater's (1988) or Karasek and Theorell's (1990) models of job quality were used directly in this study, several of the items, or similar ones, were employed. This research will therefore address the issue of job quality by not only assessing wages and benefits, but will also determine whether any of the *nonwag*e job characteristics suggested by Rosenthal; Jencks, Perman, and Rainwater; and Karasek and Theorell were applicable to the work experience of the low-income part-time elder workers in this study.

Some of these same job characteristics have been incorporated into recent discussions of "good" versus "bad" part-time employment. As mentioned previously, "bad" part-time employment, akin to Old Concept (Kahne 1985) or secondary part-time employment (Tilly 1996, 1992a, and 1992b) has been characterized as providing low wages and few or no benefits; little or no job security; fewer training opportunities; and little or no opportunity for career advancement or promotions.

While fully acknowledging the demand side or employer-driven reasons for the expansion of contingent work, presented by Tilly (1996, 1992a, and 1992b), Kahne (1994, 1992, and 1985), and duRivage (1992), Blank (1997) reminds us that some employers provide nonstandard labor contracts because employees want them. In the case of highly skilled mothers with young children at home, employers may be simply responding to the needs of this group of employees. Further, on the demand side, some employers use non-standard contracts to screen workers for full-time permanent positions.

Blank (1997) further points out the supply-side reasons why some workers explicitly seek nonstandard work contracts, reasons which have been downplayed somewhat in recent evaluations of part-time and other contingent work arrangements. According to Blank (1995), some workers want the more limited hours and greater flexibility in scheduling provided by nonstandard employment arrangements. Other workers like the greater variety and independence which some nonstandard work contracts provide. Further, some of these workers can use nonstandard jobs as a way to search for full-time jobs.

Given these factors, Blank maintains that "contingent jobs cannot be immediately categorized as 'good jobs' or 'bad jobs,'" a point that she also made in some of her earlier work (Blank 1990). Further, among other research questions she poses, she recommends that research should be done which addresses the extent to which low wages and fringe benefits, which characterize many contingent jobs, are offset in the minds of workers by other advantages these jobs might offer.

In other words, as Blank suggested in 1990, and similar to the work of Jencks, Perman, and Rainwater (1988), what are some of the *nonwage* characteristics of work which also contribute heavily to overall job quality? Or as Blank indicated in 1995, what are some of the "compensating differentials" involved in part-time, temporary, and independent contracting jobs that can be balanced against their low wages and minimal fringe benefits?

Drawing then on the work of Friedmann and Havighurst (1954); Karasek and Theorell (1990); Rosenthal (1989); Jencks, Perman, and Rainwater (1988); Kahne (1994, 1992, and 1985); Tilly (1996, 1992a, and 1992b); Blank (1995, 1990); and Polivka and Nardone (1989), we will use the following criteria to make an overall assessment about whether the part-time jobs that our study participants received were mostly "good" or "bad" part-time jobs.

First we will assess what our respondents were looking for in a part-time position and whether the kinds of jobs they received were the kinds of jobs they wanted. Were they working part-time voluntarily? Further, we will evaluate their job security; their opportunity for career advancement and training; and whether or not they received wages and benefits prorated to those of equivalent full-time workers. We will assess whether our respondents felt their working conditions were hazardous or required too much physical exertion. We will determine whether they had predictable working hours and whether these hours involved shift or overtime work. We will assess their job satisfaction, including the degree to which they could use existing skills or acquire new ones. We will also evaluate the extent to which our respondents reported developing meaningful social relationships and had meaningful life experiences at work.

While not explicitly enumerated among the job-quality characteristics mentioned above, we will also assess the extent to which elders felt discriminated against at work because of age, gender, race, national origin, or because they worked part-time. Because the literature indicates that elder workers are not homogeneous either with respect to their desires or their actual experiences of part-time work, we will assess whether or not the experience of part-time employment varied, depending on the age, gender, race, or SCSEP status of our elder respondents.

Chapter Three
Our Approach to Learning about Low-Income Older Adults Who Worked Part-Time

Our analysis of the experiences of older part-time employees in the Greater Philadelphia area was premised on the importance of using a variety of data sources. As a result, there were three major phases of research activity.

Phase I involved a secondary analysis of older worker case-record files maintained at four senior employment and placement programs in the Greater Philadelphia metropolitan area. This stage focused on obtaining basic background data about all part-time job placements made by these agencies during the period July 1, 1987, through June 30, 1988, hereafter referred to as fiscal 1987. A total of 613 cases were eventually analyzed. After consultation with agency staff, this time frame was chosen to balance the need for older workers to have worked long enough to make informed assessments about their part-time work experiences, but not so long that a substantial proportion might no longer be employed.

In Phase II, a combination of semistructured in-person and telephone interviews was conducted with older workers from each of the four senior employment and placement programs whose records had been subject to the secondary analysis during Phase I. A total of 265 such individuals were ultimately interviewed between July 1989 and January 1990. At that time, 164 were working part-time, 21 were working full-time, and 80 were unemployed.

Phase III consisted of face-to-face open-ended interviews with twelve key informants (program directors and other staff) from each of the four senior employment and placement programs. These key informants were asked to elaborate on the dominant issues and problems which surfaced during the course of placing low-income elders in part-time employment.

Preliminary Activity

Prior to the construction of the research protocol, a series of meetings was held with directors and staff of the four participating senior employment and placement programs. These discussions were helpful in identifying the sample of workers who would participate in the study and in developing the survey instruments. A review of the literature on older workers specifically, and employment generally, as well as discussions with acknowledged experts in the fields of employment and aging, were essential in identifying major variables to be incorporated in the analysis. A review of related research also served to isolate a range of standardized scales and other indices that could be adopted as is or modified for use in this study.

Senior Community Service Employment Program

Three of the study placement programs were part of the Senior Community Service Employment Program, referred to as SCSEP, which is a national employment and training program, authorized under Title V of the Older Americans Act, and administered by the Office of Special Targeted Programs, Employment and Training Administration, U.S. Department of Labor. This program, now 30 years old, originated in 1964 as Operation Mainstream under the Office of Economic Opportunity and was later incorporated in the early 1970s into the Older Americans Act as the Senior Community Service Employment Program. It is the only workforce development program focused exclusively on older men and women ("Why Support SCSEP? It Works!" 1995). At the same time, it is a relatively small, obscure program, unknown to many in the communities where programs are located, with minimal expenditures on public relations efforts (Freedman 1994).

Total federal funds allocated for this program in fiscal 1987 were $336 million. They increased to $367 million by fiscal 1990, and were authorized at $410.5 million for fiscal 1994. For fiscal 1995 a recision reduced the authorization to $396 million, with clear indications that further reductions would occur for fiscal 1996 (personal communication, Charles Atkinson, Chief, Division of Older Worker Programs, U.S. Department of Labor, July 28, 1995). About one-fifth of the funds are distributed to employment projects sponsored by all state and territorial governments and about four-fifths to ten national nonprofit organizations (Bass, Quinn, and Burkhauser 1995). At the time of this research, these organizations included: Asociacion Nacional pro Personas Mayores, the National Caucus Center on Black Aged, Inc., National Council on Aging, American Association of Retired Persons, National Council of Senior Citizens, National Urban League, Inc., Green Thumb, Inc., National Asian Pacific Center on Aging, the U.S. Forest Service, and the National Indian Council on Aging. Funding supported 64,933 enrollees in 1990 (Kilborn 1990). By 1993 enrollment had increased to 65,345, but dropped in 1994 to 64,407. Authorized enrollment for fiscal 1996 has dropped to 61,071.

The goals of the SCSEP programs are to create part-time community-service jobs in both the public and private nonprofit sectors for able-bodied elders, 55 and over, with family income of no more than 125 percent of the poverty levels established and periodically updated by the U.S. Department of Health and Human Services. Income eligibility ceilings in 1987–88 were $7,850 if the individual was single, and $10,525 if married. By 1996, eligibility ceilings had increased to $9,675 for single individuals, and $12,950 for married couples. While local programs have wide latitude in the kinds of work assignments they can provide, most job placements are in clerical and service positions. Jobs are in programs for children, the aged, and the disabled; schools, parks, and transportation services; and literacy, conservation, and restoration projects.

Other than an annual physical, Workmen's Compensation, and any other benefits required by state law, no specific benefits are mandated. However, benefits such as annual leave, sick leave, holidays, and health insurance are allowable, as long as they are administered uniformly to all enrollees in a project or subproject (*Federal Register* July 19, 1985, p. 29613). While sponsors are also encouraged to place as many enrollees in unsubsidized positions as possible, with an overall program goal since 1985 of around 22 percent, there is considerable variation from one program to the next. The majority of enrollees, termed "career enrollees" by Freedman (1994, 63), are placed in subsidized employment, typically working 20 to 25 hours a week and not exceeding 1,300 hours a year. These enrollees are paid at minimum-wage rates—either the existing federal or state minimum wage, whichever is higher. Income earned from subsidized employment is taxed. While the degree to which job-related counseling and training are provided varies considerably across program sites, programs as a whole have been criticized for devoting only minimal attention to training (Schultz, Borowski, and Crown 1991; Doeringer 1990b; and Sandell 1988).

Participants in the Research

All adults 55 and over who had been placed by the four different placement agencies in fiscal 1987 were included in the sampling frame. The participating older adult job-placement programs were:

a. *The Older Workers Program of the Center for Career Services, Jewish Employment and Vocational Services (JEVS)*, an SCSEP program that assists people aged 55 and over in reentering the job market by providing job-search training and placement services.

b. *Project Ayuda of the Asociacion Nacional por Personas Mayores*, also an SCSEP program, provides part-time subsidized employment in community-service work in public and private nonprofit agencies, as well as training skills, job development, and eventual placement in part-time or full-time work outside the program.

c. *Senior Employment and Educational Services, Inc. (SEES)*, a private, nonprofit placement service in Philadelphia exclusively for workers 50 years of age or older, which is supported by grants from corporate and other private funders. This agency receives no government funding.

d. *The Senior Community Service Employment Program of the Delaware County Office of Services for the Aging (COSA)*, an SCSEP program, operated by the Delaware County Area on Aging, located in Media, PA. This program also has a Job Bank for elders who are not part of the SCSEP program. Some of these individuals were also included in the study.

These agencies were purposely chosen to reflect the range of agencies, both public and private, assisting low-income elders in securing part-time employment in the Philadelphia metropolitan area.

Although two of the agencies—SEES and COSA—did place some middle-income workers, clear majorities of their placements were for the low-income, working-class elderly—the group of particular interest in this study. Variations in demographic characteristics of the older persons served was of particular interest, especially differences in gender, age, and race/ethnicity. We were also interested in comparing results for those elders who were SCSEP enrollees and those who were not.

The sampling frame for Phase I—the analysis of agency case-record data—consisted of 613 cases, representing all elders placed in part-time positions from the four placement agencies in fiscal 1987. These elders had been placed in part-time positions in a variety of mostly semiskilled and unskilled positions, including clerical, factory, bookkeeping, sales, custodian, companion, transportation, and entry-level administration slots. Elders placed through the Center for Career Services of the Jewish Employment and Vocational Services and Project Ayuda of the Asociacion Nacional pro Personas Mayores were all SCSEP employees, placed almost exclusively in subsidized positions. While the Delaware County Office of Services for the Aging made mostly SCSEP placements, SEES placed elders exclusively in non-SCSEP, unsubsidized positions. In addition, as indicated above, all elders placed in fiscal 1987 through Delaware County's Job Bank program, which placed middle-income elders, were also included in the sampling frame.

During Phase II, intensive, semistructured interviews were conducted with systematic random samples drawn from placement lists of all part-time placements made during fiscal 1987 by three of the four participating agencies. Because we wished to include as many Hispanics as possible, we did not sample from Project Ayuda but approached all elders placed by that agency in fiscal 1987.

The majority of face-to-face interviews were conducted in these elders' homes at times convenient to them, though about a quarter were conducted at the respondents' job sites. A total of 164 interviews were completed with elders employed in part-time jobs at the time of data collection. Of these 164 interviews, 12 (7.3 percent) were conducted by telephone because of scheduling difficulties.

In order to obtain interviews with 150 elders working part-time—a minimum judged necessary to comfortably accommodate analyses with breakdowns by age, gender, race/ethnicity, and SCSEP status—substantially larger samples had to be drawn and a greater number of interviews conducted during Phase II than originally anticipated. This was necessary because of those elders who agreed to be interviewed, 38.2 percent (101 respondents) were discovered to be no longer working part-time at the time of their interview; 80 were unemployed and 21 were working full-time. Excluding Project Ayuda, a 30 percent systematic random sample was drawn initially from the other three agencies; this percentage was ultimately increased to a 50 percent systematic random sample for the reason just cited.

A final participation rate of 63.5 percent was achieved, with individual agency response rates during Phase II ranging from a high of 68.9 percent to a low of 58.7 percent. This represents, in fact, a technically correct yet conservative measure of the response rate in that 5 persons who were sampled were found to be deceased, 13 were in extremely poor health and could not be interviewed, 17 were ineligible to participate because they said they had not been placed in part-time employment by the placement agency, and 78 could not be reached because they had moved, no longer had a telephone, or had a missing agency record. If "active declines" alone (39) are used to calculate response totals, the study's aggregate rate for completed interviews (based on a corrected potential interviewee pool of 304 persons) increased to 87.2 percent. There were no significant differences among the four agencies in terms of the number of part-time, full-time, and unemployed respondents interviewed.

Part-time employed persons were paid $10.00 for their participation at the time of the interview, whereas unemployed and full-time employed older adults, who responded to a smaller number of questionnaire items, were paid $5.00 for their participation.

As indicated earlier, the reason for drawing substantially larger samples was the fact that close to 40 percent of those elders reached who agreed to participate were no longer employed part-time when interviewed, but were either unemployed (30.3 percent) or working full-time (7.9 percent). Interviewing these two categories of elder workers was costly in terms of time, money, and effort; however, since these elders had also been originally placed in part-time positions in fiscal 1987, their subsequent work experiences were considered essential for gaining a more comprehensive understanding of the elder part-time work experience. While the unemployed and full-timers were initially interviewed in person, because of time and costs, telephone interviews were adopted midway through the interviewing phase of the project. In the end, 64 percent (51 of 80) of those unemployed and 37 percent of the full-timers (8 of 21) were interviewed by telephone.

The Study Protocol
The following provides more detailed information about the three study instruments.

1. The Agency Case-Record Instrument
This one-page instrument contained variables which were collected on a regular basis by the four job-placement programs. Areas of information included were:

a. Sociodemographic characteristics of the older worker (e.g., gender, race, age, education, marital status, living arrangements, public-assistance status, handicap status, whether they spoke English or not, and family income level);
b. Characteristics of the job held immediately prior to coming to the job placement agency (e.g., type, hourly wage, number of hours worked, length of employment); and
c. Characteristics of the job in which the older person was placed (e.g., type, hourly wage, number of hours worked).

This instrument required approximately 10–15 minutes to complete. Data collection was carried out at each of the four agency sites by agency staff, trained by the principal investigators.

2. The Older Adult Interview Instrument
This comprehensive 128-item instrument was designed to gather detailed information about older workers, whether part-time or full-time employed, or unemployed. Both English and Spanish versions of this questionnaire were developed. Six pretest interviews were done in July of 1989, with respondents selected from three of the four placement agencies (COSA, SEES, AYUDA). Participants used in

the pretest were all working part-time, having been placed in their positions sometime during 1988–89. Minor revisions were made in the protocol as a result of these interviews. Not all respondents answered all 128 questions. The 47 questions answered by all interviewees, regardless of current employment status, covered the following basic areas:

a. Experience with the job-placement program
b. Employment history
c. Characteristics of the longest job held
d. Extensive demographic and other background data, including a series of questions around social support and family contact, health status, life satisfaction, and retirement decisions and attitudes

For those who were either unemployed or working full-time at the time of their interview, a small subset of questions was asked. Those unemployed were asked a series of questions about their last job and job-seeking plans for the future. Those working full-time were asked a series of questions about their job, including information about the type of job, earnings, benefits, and whether or not they had obtained the job through the placement agency.

Those working part-time at the time of their interview were asked a subset of 60 questions, addressing the following areas:

1. Structural and functional characteristics of their part-time jobs
2. Their perception of discrimination and marginality in their part-time positions
3. Intragenerational and intergenerational workplace relationships
4. Job satisfaction and commitment

This interview required approximately one hour to administer. It consisted of a mix of open-ended and forced-choice questions. While comprised primarily of questions constructed especially for this study, a series of previously developed scales were used as well.

Table 1 presents the specific scales which were developed by others and used in this research in either original or modified form.

Table 1 Previously Developed Scales Used in the Older Worker Interviews

Substantive Issue	Source
Reasons for job departure	Irelan, Rabin, and Schwab 1987
Person recommending job departure	Irelan, Rabin, and Schwab 1987
Reasons for needing a job	Centaur Associates, 1986
Kind of business/industry	Quinn and Staines 1979
Fringe benefits list	Quinn and Staines 1979
Characteristics of job	Quinn and Staines 1979
Discrimination on the job	Quinn and Staines 1979
Work attitudes	Goodwin 1972
Job satisfaction	Quinn and Staines 1979
Social support/family contact	Monk, Kaye, and Diamond 1986
Attitudes about work and retirement	Irelan, Rabin, and Schwab 1987
Life satisfaction	Duke University 1978

3. The Job-Placement Agency Staff Interviews

This instrument was comprised of a series of ten open-ended questions aimed at gauging staff views about the part-time employment experience of older adults. The instrument, which was administered through face-to-face interviews with staff at each of the four sites, required approximately one to two hours to complete. Areas addressed included: older-worker expectations; job satisfaction; discrimination in the workplace; characteristics of successful placements; common problems observed; the benefits, if any, of unionization of older part-timers; and the growth of agencies making temporary job placements for workers across a wide age span. These data have been interspersed throughout the remaining chapters, where relevant.

Data from the three sources described above were supplemented by a series of case vignettes which research interviewers compiled, based on their observations and discussions during Phase II interviews. These "snapshot" summaries of the experiences and expectations of older adults seeking part-time employment provide first-hand experiences to further elaborate quantitative results.

Data Collection

Case-record data were collected from March through May 1989. Data collection was carried out by agency staff, following several sessions of training led by the principal investigators. The expert knowledge of agency staff about case-record data-collection procedures served to expedite this process to a significant degree. Older adult interviews began in July 1989 and continued through early 1990. Interviews with agency staff were carried out after Phase I and II data had been collected, during the winter of 1990.

Phase II procedures entailed the mailing of letters of explanation to all those older persons who had been drawn randomly from agency placement lists. These individuals were advised of the nature of the study, the fact that their participation was voluntary, that all information obtained would be treated confidentially, and that they would be compensated financially for their willingness to participate in the research.

Field interviewers, who were current or former MSS students at the Graduate School of Social Work and Social Research at Bryn Mawr College, underwent approximately six hours of orientation and training in the administration of the older-worker interview schedule. Coders were trained in a similar manner. The same protocol was used for all interviews, but as mentioned previously, a reduced number of items were included for the unemployed and full-time workers. Spanish-speaking interviewers performed all interviews with older adults placed in jobs by Project Ayuda, using the Spanish-version protocol. All face-to-face interviews began with the reading of a brief explanation of the nature and intent of the study and a request from the interviewer that the interviewee sign a Statement of Explanation and Consent Form. Assurances of confidentiality and anonymity were given at this time, as well as a review of the voluntary nature of the study.

Data Analysis

All collected case-record data (Phase I) and interview data (Phase II) were numerically coded and then entered into computerized data files. Prior to statistical analysis, selected index items were recoded in order to insure consistency in terms of the direction of response choice values. Descriptive statistics and frequency distributions were computed as well as Pearson's correlations, t-tests, chi squares, analysis of variance, and multiple regressions. Reliability coefficients (Cronbach's alpha) were computed for the study's composite measures. In order to maximize readability, the presentation of findings that follows is made in large part without reference to specific statistical procedures or detailed statistical results.

Chapter Four
Who Were the Low-Income Older Part-Timers?

A Note of Explanation

As indicated in chapter 3, there were two primary sources of information for this analysis: (1) case-record data on 613 older adults who were placed in part-time positions by the four senior employment and placement programs we studied; and (2) interview data from 265 elder workers from each of these four programs. This chapter and chapter 6 draw on a combination of case-record and interview data. Chapters 5 and 7 through 13 analyze interview data only. Further, chapters 5 and 6 compare interview data from those working part-time (N=164) and those unemployed (N=80) at the time of their interviews. Chapters 7 through 11 focus only on the 164 elders who were still employed part-time when interviewed. In chapters 5 through 11, we provide within-group comparisons of the part-timers by age, gender, race/ethnicity, and SCSEP status for all key variables.

As is common with case-record data, there were varying amounts of missing data for some of these variables. When there was more than 20 percent missing data from any one variable, we noted this fact. In those instances, some caution should be used in interpreting the results. When significant differences between two groups of participants are noted in the text, the reader can assume that difference is at least at the $p < .05$ level. Lastly, data from the third information source—open-ended interviews with key personnel from each agency—are used in subsequent chapters primarily as an aid in the interpretation of some of the results.

As described in chapter 3, we remind the reader that some of those elders interviewed were no longer employed part-time at the time of their interviews. At that time, of the 265 interviewees, 164

(62 percent) were working part-time, 80 (30 percent) were unemployed, and 21 (8 percent) were working full-time. Chapters 12 and 13 specifically address the experiences of the unemployed and full-time workers who were identified during the course of our research.

Profiling the Older Part-Time Worker

This section is divided into four parts. Part 1 compares basic demographic data for the sample of 265 interviewed elder workers with all 613 elders placed by the four agencies in part-time positions in fiscal 1987. Part 1 comparisons are based entirely on case-record data. Part 2 includes a comparison of selected demographic characteristics of SCSEP enrollees nationwide in 1987–88 with all SCSEP enrollees from the three placement agencies in this study which placed SCSEP enrollees. Using interview data only, part 3 compares the 164 elders who were working part-time with the 80 elders who were unemployed at the time of their interviews. These analyses compare basic demographic and perceived health-status data, as well as indicators of overall happiness and life satisfaction.

Since almost one-third of the interviewees were not working at the time they were interviewed, we felt it important to determine whether differences in demographic characteristics, prior work history, or experiences with the job-placement agency distinguished the unemployed elders from those still working part-time at the time of their interview. Part 4 covers most of the same background variables as part 3, but focuses on within-group comparisons of the part-timers only. Chapter 4 closes with a brief summary of our observations of the characteristics of older part-timers.

Part 1: Comparison of Demographic Characteristics of All Employment Program Participants (N=613) and All Interviewed Respondents (N=265) for Fiscal 1987

Interviewees were similar to program participants on a number of characteristics. Over two-thirds of each were female. Somewhat over a third of each had less than a high-school education. Roughly the same percentages had high-school diplomas. While small but equal percentages of each (between 6 percent and 7 percent) had a college education or beyond, somewhat more of the interviewees (22 percent vs. 12.5 percent) had between one and three years of college.

Overall, then, the majority of both groups were female and had a high-school education or more.

There were significant differences between the two groups in terms of age and marital status. While the mean age for all program participants was almost 65 years, interviewees tended to be somewhat older—almost 67 years on the average. Likewise, while half of all program participants were between the ages of 54 and 64, only slightly over a third of the interviewees were in that younger age range. By contrast, slightly over half of the interviewees were between ages 65 and 74, compared with slightly more than four in ten program participants. Fewer than one in ten of the program participants and interviewees were in the oldest age group—aged 75 to 86. Although the interviewees were older, on average, the overwhelming majority from both groups (in each case 93 percent) reported no restrictions in the kinds of jobs they could perform—a good indicator that this was an able-bodied group of elders.

In terms of marital status, there were also significant differences between the two groups. While about a third of each group were married, more of the program participants were single (21 percent) than were the interviewees (7 percent). On the other hand, more of the interviewees were widowed, separated, or divorced than were program participants. There were also significant differences between the two groups in terms of race/ethnicity. While slightly over a third of each group were white, significantly more of the program participants were African American (47 percent vs. 41 percent). On the other hand, more of the interviewees were Hispanic (18 percent vs. 12 percent of the program participants), which accounts for a significantly greater percentage of the interviewees (20 percent vs. 15 percent) having limited English-speaking ability. Very small percentages of each were Asian. Overall, then, close to two-thirds of both program participants and interviewees were of minority backgrounds.

The majority of both groups (over 80 percent in each case) were also heads of households. Almost 60 percent of each group lived alone, while a third of each lived in two-person households. Only about one-tenth of each group lived in a household with three or more persons. At the same time, finances were limited. Although less than 12 percent of either group received public assistance, the mean family income for all program participants was $7,273 and for interviewees, $7,302. Because both distributions were skewed, median income figures provide a better representation of average income. In this case, the median income for all program participants was $5,358, and $5,766 for interviewees.

Finally, there were no significant differences between the numbers in each group who were SCSEP workers—slightly more than half of all enrollees and interviewees. Over 95 percent of all program participants and interviewees who were SCSEP enrollees were placed in subsidized positions.

Part 2: Comparison of Selected Demographic Statistics for All SCSEP Enrollees Nationwide with SCSEP Program Participants (N=347) in This Study

Of the 613 elders placed in part-time positions by the four agencies, 57 percent (347) were SCSEP employees. Annual enrollee statistics on SCSEP programs nationwide are available from the Office of Special Targeted Programs, Employment and Training Administration, U.S. Department of Labor. Selected characteristics for 1987–88 (fiscal 1987) are included in Table 2. According to these statistics, 67,910 individuals were enrolled in these programs during fiscal 1987. Of these, about 70 percent were female. About 63 percent were white, about 24 percent were African American, about 9 percent were Hispanic, and about 3 percent were Asian. Almost one-half had less than a high-school education; about one-third had finished high school; and the remaining one-sixth had some college or more. Twenty percent were between the ages of 55 and 59; about 29 percent, between 60 and 64; 25 percent, between 65 and 69; and about 26 percent, over 70. The mean hourly wage for all enrollees was $3.51, and 22 percent were placed in unsubsidized employment.

While we did not recruit our sample to be representative of SCSEP program participants nationwide, it is instructive to see how the population of enrollees from the three study placement sites that placed SCSEP enrollees compared with the population of national enrollees for fiscal 1987. As presented in Table 2, there were 347 SCSEP enrollees placed in part-time positions by the three programs. As was true for the SCSEP programs nationwide, about three-quarters were female. The education and age distributions were also reasonably similar. About 46 percent of this study's enrollees, compared to 49 percent of all SCSEP enrollees, had less than an eleventh-grade education. About a third of each group were high-school graduates, and close to 20 percent of each had some college or beyond. Close to half of each group were between the ages of 55 and 64. Slightly more of the study enrollees were between the ages of 65 and 69 than enrollees nationwide, and slightly more of the national SCSEP enrollees were over 70.

Table 2 Comparison of Selective Demographic Statistics (1987–88) of SCSEP Enrollees Nationwide with SCSEP Study Participants[1]

Variable	National Enrollees		Program Participants	
	Number	%	Number	%
Sex				
Male	21,006	30.9	93	26.8
Female	46,904	69.1	254	73.2
TOTAL	67,910	100.0	347	100.0
Race/Ethnicity				
Asian	2,175	3.2	14	4.0
African American	16,191	23.8	176	50.7
Hispanic	5,898	8.7	69	19.9
White	42,599	62.7	86	24.8
Other	1,017	1.5	2	0.6
TOTAL	67,880	100.0	347	100.0
Education				
8th Grade or Less	18,862	27.8	81	23.3
9–11th Grade	14,467	21.3	80	23.1
High School	23,045	33.9	121	35.0
1–3 Years College	8,099	11.9	51	14.7
College Degree or More	3,437	5.1	13	3.8
TOTAL	67,910	100.0	346	100.0
Age				
55–59	13,604	20.0	65	18.7
60–64	19,399	28.6	96	27.7
65–69	17,057	25.1	109	31.4
70–74	10,573	15.6	46	13.3
75 +	7,277	10.7	31	8.9
TOTAL	67,910	100.0	347	100.0

[1]Senior Community Service Employment Program, Quarter Ending 6/30/88—National Summary—All Sponsors—Enrollment Levels.
Total percentages are rounded.

The one area where the study SCSEP enrollees differed dramatically from national SCSEP enrollees was in minority composition. Whereas almost two-thirds of the national enrollees were white, three-quarters of the study SCSEP enrollees were minorities. There were two times as many African Americans, two times as many Hispanics, and about equal and very small numbers of Asians in the study SCSEP sample.

Average hourly wages for each group were similar: $3.51 for national SCSEP enrollees, and $3.53 for the study enrollees, both of which were close to the 1987 minimum federal and Pennsylvania wage in 1987 of $3.35 an hour. However, while 78 percent of SCSEP enrollees nationwide were placed in subsidized positions in 1987, almost all of the study SCSEP enrollees—98 percent—were placed in subsidized positions.

It should be noted that between fiscal 1987 and 1995 (the last year for which enrollment data were available), basic demographic data about national SCSEP enrollees have remained fairly constant in terms of gender, race, education, and age, with minor fluctuations of no more than three or four percentage points. Placement rates in unsubsidized employment have fluctuated between 21.7 percent in fiscal 1990 to a high of 27.3 percent in fiscal 1995. Reflecting changes in the federal minimum wage, the mean hourly wage increased to $4.41 in fiscal 1995.

Part 3: Comparison of Those Unemployed (N=80) and Those Working Part-Time (N=164) at the Time of the Interview

There were no statistically significant differences between the unemployed and part-timers in terms of gender, minority status, age, marital status, education, and income. As presented in Table 3, about two-thirds from each group were female. Minorities far outnumbered whites, with African Americans the largest minority—around 40 percent of each group. Hispanics constituted 14 percent of the unemployed group and 22 percent of the part-timers. The percentage of Asians was very small for each group. Somewhat over one-third of each group was white. The mean age of the part-timers was 67 (SD=5.5); the mean age of the unemployeds was 66 (SD=5.5). About two-thirds from both groups were 65 and over. The modal

Table 3 Comparison of Demographic Characteristics of
Unemployed and Part-Time Interviewees

	Unemployed N = 80		Part-timers N = 164	
	Number	%	Number	%
Sex				
Male	23	28.8	55	33.5
Female	57	71.3	109	66.5
TOTAL	80	100.0*	164	100.0
Race/Ethnicity				
Asian	1	1.3	1	.6
Hispanic	11	14.1	36	22.2
African American	33	42.3	65	40.1
White	33	42.3	60	37.0
TOTAL	78	100.0	162	100.0*
Age				
54–59	12	15.0	14	8.5
60–64	16	20.0	40	24.4
65–69	35	43.8	74	45.1
70–74	12	15.0	17	10.4
75–86	5	6.2	19	11.6
TOTAL	80	100.0	164	100.0
	x = 66.0		x = 67.1	
	S.D. = 5.5		S.D. = 5.5	
	Med. = 67		Med. = 66	
Marital Status				
Single	10	12.5	7	4.3
Married	24	30.0	60	36.6
Widowed	28	35.0	58	35.4
Separated/Divorced	18	22.5	39	23.8
TOTAL	80	100.0	164	100.0*
Education				
8th Grade or Less	16	20.5	39	23.8
9–11th Grade	10	12.8	27	16.5
12th Grade	32	41.0	55	33.5
Trade/Professional School	4	5.1	16	9.8
Some College	13	16.7	17	10.4
4 Years College or More	3	3.8	10	6.1
TOTAL	78	100.0*	164	100.0*
Total Family Income				
Less than $5,000	19	25.0	25	15.9
$5,000–$9,000	26	34.2	57	36.3
$10,000–$14,999	12	15.8	38	24.2
$15,000–$19,999	8	10.5	17	10.8
$20,000–$24,999	11	14.5	20	12.7
TOTAL	76	100.0	157	100.0*

*Total percentages are rounded.

category—ages 65 to 69—contained roughly 45 percent of each group. Only 15 percent of the unemployed and 8.5 percent of the part-timers were younger than 60 years of age. Around one-fifth of each group were aged 70 and over.

About one-third of the part-timers and unemployeds were married. Somewhat more of the unemployed were single, though about one-third of each group were widowed and about one-fifth, separated or divorced. On average, the part-timers had three children, while the unemployed had two children. Even though about 40 percent of each group lived alone, members of both groups had a good deal of contact with their children—84 percent of the unemployed and 82 percent of the part-timers spoke to one or more of their children two or more times a week. Not only was their frequency of contact with their children high, but over three-quarters of each group reported having friends with whom they felt close or whom they saw regularly. As with their children, over 80 percent either saw or spoke to at least one friend at least once a week.

While about three-quarters of both the unemployed and part-timers had a high-school education or less, there was a statistical trend, falling just short of significance, for the unemployed to have more education overall. About 20 percent of the unemployed and 16 percent of the part-timers had some college or more. While somewhat more of the part-timers (10 percent) than those unemployed (5 percent) had *completed* trade or professional education, about 44 percent of both part-timers and the unemployed had *attended* a trade or professional school, with an average attendance of about a year and a half.

In spite of the fact that the part-timers were working, there were no statistical differences between the unemployed and part-timers in terms of total family income. The average income category for both groups was between $5,000 and $9,000 annually. It should be noted that the federal poverty level for a family of one between July 1987 and early February 1989 was $5,500, and for a family of two, $7,400. A sizable proportion of the program participants and interviewees, therefore, had incomes near or below the poverty level for 1987–89. More of the unemployed (25 percent) reported annual family incomes of less than $5,000 per annum, compared to about 16 percent of the part-timers. While there were slightly more of the unemployed who had incomes over $20,000 per annum (14.5 percent vs. 12.7 percent), almost one-quarter of the part-timers, but only 16 percent of the unemployed, had incomes of between $10,000 and $15,000 per annum. Close to one-third of each group received a private pension—32 percent of both the unemployed and the part-timers, figures fairly comparable to those cited in other studies in the 1980s of older workers (Mitchell 1988; 9 to 5 1987). Given the low total family income, however, pension income for the majority of study elders was quite small.

To round out the picture of overall economic well-being, it is useful to briefly consider the number of government benefits members of each group were receiving. Over three-quarters of the respondents in each group were receiving Social Security and about 60 percent of each were receiving Medicare; 10 percent in each group received Medicaid. Over 90 percent of the participants in each group did not receive the following benefits: public assistance, Veterans Administration pensions, Supplemental Security Income, rent subsidies, or subsidized housing. Likewise, none of the unemployed received unemployment compensation, which is generally true for part-timers, whatever their age (duRivage 1992; Callaghan and Hartmann 1991; International Labor Office 1989). Regarding SCSEP status, significantly more of the part-timers (60 percent) were SCSEP enrollees than the unemployed elders (45 percent).

Less than one-third of each group reported any serious health problems. Of those reporting problems, roughly equal percentages from each group reported arthritis (25 percent of each); cardiac problems (20 percent of each); and high blood pressure, somewhat over 10 percent of each. The relationship of health status and aging to job performance is complex, depending to a large extent on differences in job requirements and individual variations in capacity (Sterns and Miklos, 1995). However, the fact that a relatively small percentage of either group of elders cited major health difficulties comes as no surprise (Ruhm 1990). *Healthy People 2000*, a comprehensive national effort reviewing the health status of U.S. citizens, indicated that 80 percent of those aged 65–68 and 78 percent of those aged 69 to 74 reported not being limited in the *amount* or *kind* of major activities they could perform (U.S. Department of Health and Human Services 1990).

Two final areas compared were the subjective assessment of physical health and life satisfaction. Although about two-thirds within each group did not perceive themselves as limited in the *amount* of work they could do, significantly more of the unemployed (74 percent) than part-timers (60 percent) viewed themselves as limited in the *kind* of work they could perform. While the elders in both groups saw themselves in good health relative to their peers, the unemployed reported significantly more worry about their physical health and saw themselves as having somewhat less energy than the part-timers. It should be noted that in the latter assessment, elders in both groups viewed themselves as having at least average energy—the part-timers only more so.

Significant differences also emerged between the two groups in terms of their assessment of life satisfaction. Although elders in both groups expressed some reservations about the way they were living, the part-timers rated their satisfaction in the "somewhat satisfactory" range, as compared to the "somewhat unsatisfactory" range for the unemployed. Likewise, in terms of overall happiness, the part-timers, on average, rated themselves in the "somewhat happy" range, while the unemployed rated themselves in the "somewhat unhappy" range, a difference that was statistically significant. This somewhat tempered view was further expressed in the elders' ratings of "overall satisfaction" with life in general, which for both the unemployed and part-timers was rated in the "fair" range. While limited to elders 55–64, Davis (1991) found that higher family income ($15,000 or more per annum) was consistently associated with higher reported life satisfaction. Given the generally low incomes of our respondents, our findings were not surprising.

Part 4: Within-Group Comparisons of Selected Background Characteristics of Part-Time Elder Workers (N=164)

Looking first at the relationship of age, race/ethnicity, gender, SCSEP, and marital status, although the majority of each racial/ethnic group was 65 years of age and over (61 percent of Hispanics, 54 percent of African Americans, and 83 percent of whites), significantly more of the whites were over 65. In addition, significantly more of the men than women (80 percent vs. 61 percent) were 65 and older. Almost twice as many men (33 percent) than women (17 percent) were 70 years and over.

Almost all of the Hispanic part-timers (97 percent) were SCSEP enrollees, compared to 56 percent of African Americans and 40 percent of whites. SCSEP enrollees as a whole were significantly more likely to be Hispanic (37 percent) or African American (38 percent) than white (25 percent), and to be female (65 percent) than male (35 percent). All but one of the SCSEP part-timers were in subsidized positions.

Likewise, although there were no significant differences in marital status by age or SCSEP status, men were two times more likely to be married than women (62 percent vs. 24 percent); whites (45 percent) and Hispanics (47 percent) were also almost twice as likely to be married as African Americans (25 percent). It is therefore not surprising that a much larger percentage of women (48 percent) than men (29 percent), and African Americans (43 percent) and whites (48 percent) than Hispanics (22 percent) lived alone.

In terms of education, while there were no significant differences by age, there were significant differences by minority status, with 75 percent of the Hispanics having an eighth-grade education or less, compared to about 10 percent of the African Americans and whites. On the other hand, only 6 percent of the Hispanics, but 35 percent of the African Americans and 48 percent of the whites, completed high school; 11 percent of the Hispanics, 29 percent of the African Americans, and 30 percent of the whites had some college or more. There were no significant differences between age and education or between education and gender: about one-third of the men and women had completed high school, and about one-quarter had some college.

SCSEP enrollees had significantly less education than non-SCSEP workers: of all part-timers with an eighth-grade education or less, 85 percent were SCSEP workers. Of part-timers with a ninth- to eleventh-grade education, three-quarters were SCSEP enrollees. While about 50 percent of African Americans and whites had attended trade or professional schools, only about 20 percent of Hispanics had. There were no significant differences by sex, with close to half of the women having attended. SCSEP enrollees were also significantly less likely to have attended trade or professional schools than non-SCSEP enrollees (49 percent vs. 67 percent).

Regarding income, there were significant differences by minority status and a trend by gender. While about 22 percent of both African Americans and Hispanics had household incomes less than $5,000 per annum, only 4 percent of the whites did. On the other hand, while about two-thirds of the Hispanics and African Americans had incomes less than $10,000 per annum, over two-thirds of the whites had incomes over $10,000. Almost a third of the whites had household incomes over $15,000, compared to about a tenth of Hispanics, and about one-fifth of African Americans. Our findings, therefore, conform to the broader finding that as a whole both elderly African Americans and Hispanics (National Caucus and Center on Black Aged 1994, 1987; Garcia 1993, 1988; Murray, Khatib, and Jackson 1989) have lower incomes and are much more likely to be living in poverty than are the white elderly.

When marital status was controlled, however, the relationship between minority status and income was sustained for those who were married, but not for those who were single. As expected, there was also a strong trend for men to report the highest household incomes. On the other hand, almost 60 percent of the women, compared to almost 40 percent of the men, had household incomes less than $10,000. Likewise, when the relationship between household income and race was controlled for sex, the relationship was sustained for white men, but not for white women. Finally, as expected, household income and SCSEP status were significantly related, with 76 percent of those earning less than $5,000 being SCSEP workers.

While there were no significant differences by age, minority status, or gender between the roughly one-third of part-timers who received a private pension, significantly more of the non-SCSEP enrollees (44 percent) than SCSEP enrollees (24 percent) received a pension. Although we did not gauge the actual amount of pension income for any of our respondents, in contrast to some studies (see, for example, 9 to 5 1987), about the same number of elder female part-timers in this study received private pensions as did male part-timers. However, in accordance with available data on pension income (Christensen 1990; 9 to 5 1987; Kuriansky and Porter, forthcoming), we would expect the pensions of the males to be larger than those of the females.

While there were no significant differences by gender or SCSEP status, there were significant differences by age and by minority status in terms of the receipt of Social Security and Medicare. Significantly more whites (92 percent) than African Americans (71 percent) and Hispanics (75 percent) received Social Security. Likewise, significantly more whites (75 percent), than African Americans (56 percent) and Hispanics (47 percent) received Medicare. Even though only a small percentage of part-timers received Medicaid, of those that did, there were significantly more men than women, more Hispanics than African Americans or whites, and more SCSEP enrollees than their non-SCSEP counterparts.

Although less than one-third of part-timers reported serious health problems, among those who did, significantly more were Hispanic than African American or white. There was also a trend for a significantly higher percentage of SCSEP (33 percent) than non-SCSEP workers to report them. There were no significant differences by age or gender.

While data on the health status of the Hispanic elderly is generally sparse, what does exist suggests greater health vulnerability and poorer overall health status for Hispanics compared to other groups of the elderly (Sotomayor 1994; Sotomayor and Randolph 1988). Our results conform to this finding. Although a synthesis of the literature and demographic findings about African American elders has revealed more health debilitation for African Americans as a whole than for white elderly (Sterns and Sterns 1995; National Caucus and Center on Black Aged 1992; and Murray, Khatib, and Jackson 1989), somewhat fewer of our study's African American than white respondents reported serious health problems.

There were no significant differences by minority status, gender, age, or SCSEP status in terms of the amount of worry their health had caused them or their assessment of their energy levels relative to same-aged peers. Overall, the subgroup ratings were in the "hardly any worry" and "above average energy" ranges. However, there were significant differences by gender and minority status, but not by age and SCSEP status, in terms of how part-timers assessed their own health relative to their peers. In this instance, women rated themselves as significantly healthier than did men. Likewise, African Americans reported themselves as significantly healthier than did the Hispanics. While African Americans rated themselves solidly in the "good" range, Hispanics rated themselves only in the "fair" range, as did whites.

There were significant differences by gender, minority status, and SCSEP status, but not age, in terms of the extent of overall perceived life satisfaction. Males expressed significantly greater satisfaction than females; SCSEP enrollees, greater satisfaction than non-SCSEP enrollees; and Hispanics, greater life satisfaction than either whites or African Americans. However, the only subgroup who rated themselves higher than the overall mean for part-timers as a whole were the Hispanics, who rated themselves overall in the "good" range.

In terms of satisfaction with the way they were living, there were no significant differences by gender, age, minority, or SCSEP status. Understandably, there were significant differences by income, with those in the $15,000 and over category reporting more satisfaction than those in the $5,000 to $9,999 income bracket. Finally, in terms of overall happiness, while there were no significant differences by age or gender, there were significant differences by SCSEP status and by minority status: SCSEP enrollees and African Americans were happier than non-SCSEP enrollees and Hispanics or whites. It should be noted, however, that the mean ratings for all of the subgroup analyses were only in the "somewhat happy" range.

Part 5: Summary

In fiscal 1987, over two-thirds of the 613 program participants and the 265 interview respondents were female and about half had a high-school education or more. The majority were of minority backgrounds, primarily African American and Hispanic, lived alone, and had a median income near or below the poverty line. The reality of the poverty or near-poverty status of racial and ethnic minorities, women, and those living alone, even when they work, has been frequently noted by others (Porter 1995; Doeringer 1990b; Sum and Fogg 1990; Meier 1988; 9 to 5 1987).

The interview respondents differed significantly from the larger population of program participants in terms of age, marital status, and minority status. While half of the program participants were aged 55–64, the majority of the interviewees were over 65. While a third from each group were married, more of the interviewees were widowed and separated or divorced, while more of the program participants were single. Likewise, though the majority of both program participants and interviewees were of minority backgrounds, there were proportionately somewhat fewer African Americans and somewhat more Hispanics among the interviewees.

A comparison of SCSEP program participants nationwide and SCSEP enrollees in this study for fiscal 1987 revealed similar distributions for gender, age, and education: in other words, almost three-quarters were female; slightly over half had a high-school education or less, and slightly more than half were 65 and over. However, while almost two-thirds of the enrollees nationwide were white, somewhat over two-thirds of the study SCSEP enrollees were of minority status, mostly African Americans and Hispanics. About 20 percent of the SCSEP enrollees nationwide were placed in unsubsidized positions, compared to only a handful of the study SCSEP enrollees.

Comparisons between the unemployed and part-time interviewees revealed no significant differences by age, gender, education, minority status, marital status, and overall household income. The demographic profiles of these two groups were also similar to those comparing all program participants with all interviewees. In other words, the majority of the unemployed and part-timers were female, over age 65, of minority background, having a high-school education or more. The majority also had incomes below $9,000, were also either married or widowed, and had frequent contact with one or more of their children and/or friends.

Although both groups expressed some reservations, part-timers reported significantly higher overall satisfaction with the way they were living and somewhat higher levels of overall happiness. While fewer than one-third in either group reported serious health difficulties or saw themselves as limited in the *amount* of work they could do, more of the unemployed saw themselves as limited in the *kind* of work they could do, reported somewhat less energy overall, and worried more about their physical health.

There were clearly fewer between-group differences between the unemployed and part-timers than within-group differences among the part-timers. While the majority of part-timers were 65 years of age and over, significantly more of the whites and more of the men were over 65. Men were also two times more likely to be married than women. Almost half of the women lived alone—almost twice as many as the men. Likewise, almost a half of African Americans and whites lived alone—almost twice as many as the Hispanics.

The majority of the Hispanics, compared to 10 percent of both African Americans and whites, had less than an eighth-grade education. While about two-thirds of the African Americans and Hispanics had incomes less than $10,000 per annum, over two-thirds of the whites had incomes over $10,000 per annum. As expected, income and SCSEP status were related, with about three-quarters of those earning less than $5,000 being SCSEP workers. In addition to being poorer and having less overall education, SCSEP workers were also more likely to be of minority backgrounds and female.

Part-timers did not differ by minority status, gender, or SCSEP status in terms of the amount of worry their physical health caused them or their assessment of their energy levels relative to their own peers. They did differ by gender and minority status, but not by age or SCSEP status, in terms of how they assessed their own health relative to others their own age. Women viewed themselves as significantly healthier than men, and African Americans, significantly healthier than Hispanics. Less than one-third of the part-timers reported major health problems, with significantly more Hispanics and SCSEP workers than African Americans, whites, or non-SCSEP workers, doing so.

Overall, part-timers assessed life satisfaction in the "fair" range. However, males, SCSEP enrollees, and Hispanics expressed greater life satisfaction than women, non-SCSEP enrollees, and African Americans or whites, respectively. Overall, all subgroups rated the way they were living in the "somewhat happy" range. However, SCSEP enrollees and African Americans reported being happier than non-SCSEP, Hispanic, or white part-timers, with no significant variations by gender or age.

Chapter Five
The Previous Work Careers of Part-Time and Unemployed Elders

This chapter continues the comparison between those working part-time (N=164) and those unemployed (N=80) at the time of their interviews. The elders' experience of unemployment across their work lives is considered, followed by a description of their longest-held or "career" job. Using variables drawn from these two areas of analysis, the next section focuses on any variations among the part-timers by gender, age, race/ethnicity, or SCSEP status.

Unemployment Experiences across Their Work Lives

Elders in both groups had experienced periods of unemployment during their work lives. Although there was a statistical trend for the unemployed to have been out of work more times than the part-timers (an average of 3.7 times vs. 2.9 times), the longest period of time elders from both groups were unemployed was about five years—the same, on average, for both groups.

Characteristics of the Longest-Held or Career Job

There were again no significant differences between the unemployed and part-timers on a range of descriptive items about their longest-held or "career" job. About half of these "career jobs" for each group had been in clerical and sales positions. Close to a third of each had been in service positions, and between 14 to 18 percent from each in professional managerial, and administrative positions.

On average, respondents from both groups had worked full-time (35 hours a week or more) in their longest position, which the majority in each group had left in the late 1970s. Although the differences were not significant, the part-timers had earned somewhat more per hour than the unemployed (an hourly average of $6.58 vs.

$5.99) when they left this job. There was also a trend for the part-timers to have worked longer in this position (18.7 years vs. 16.3 years). A similar trend was noted around the average length of time out of work before coming to the agency. On average, the unemployed had been out of work slightly less time—around 4 years compared to 5.5 years for the part-timers.

In terms of the most important reason given for their leaving their career job, there was no predominant pattern. In fact, close to a quarter of the part-timers and almost 40 percent of the unemployed provided no specific reason for leaving their career jobs. Of those providing reasons, about 20 percent from each group indicated that they were either laid off or their employer went out of business. Somewhat more of the part-timers (22 percent) than the unemployed (13 percent) indicated drawing pensions or retirement benefits as a major reason. Otherwise, reasons were fairly evenly distributed across health problems, moving, and taking another job.

Overall, our results generally conform to those reported by Ruhm (1990b), based on data from all six waves of the Social Security Administration Retirement History Longitudinal Survey (RHLS). In other words, while most workers in the RHLS held a career job lasting more than fifteen years, these career jobs tended to terminate long before age 65. To quote:

By age 60, more than half of all persons had left their career jobs, but only one in nine had retired. . . . Only one 67 year old in fifteen remained in career employment, even though four in ten continued to participate in the labor force. (p. 96)

Within-Group Comparisons of the Previous Work Careers of the Part-Time Elders

Although non-SCSEP enrollees were unemployed significantly more times (almost four times vs. two times) than SCSEP enrollees, the longest period of unemployment was significantly longer for the SCSEP enrollees (an average of almost seven years vs. four years). Women's longest period of unemployment was also significantly longer than men's (six years vs. four years). While it is generally true that older women are less likely to be unemployed than older men, there is also evidence that their length of unemployment is longer (Kuriansky and Porter forthcoming), a factor noted for older workers of minority backgrounds as well (Christensen 1990). Whether women were out of the labor force voluntarily—to bear or raise children or to provide caregiving for other relatives—is not known, but these may be reasonable explanations for some of the unemployed women in this study. There were no significant differences in the longest period out of work by age or race/ethnicity.

On average, the longest job had been a full-time position, regardless of age, gender, race/ethnicity, or SCSEP status. Men and women, regardless of age, had held this job anywhere from 15 to 20 years. Those 55 to 59 years old had held this position somewhat less time than those 60 years and over. Hispanics had held their longest position significantly less time than either African Americans or whites (14.5 years vs. 21 years vs. 19 years, respectively). In terms of their final hourly wage, there was a trend for men to have earned more than women ($7.87 vs. $5.93). Our results were similar to those from the RHLS in that one of our race/ethnicity groups—Hispanics—had their career job end earlier than whites. However, the fact that men and women and African Americans all had career jobs lasting similar amounts of time is at odds with results from the RHLS, where women and all nonwhites left career jobs earlier than men and whites (Ruhm 1990b).

Although there were no significant differences by gender or age of those providing specific reasons for leaving their career job, significantly more Hispanics (50 percent) than African Americans (24 percent) or whites (31 percent) had left this job involuntarily—either because they were laid off, the employer went out of business, or the job was temporary in nature. Poor health was a factor for relatively few—12.5 percent of the Hispanics, 16 percent of the African Americans, and only 9 percent of the whites. Reaching retirement age was a factor for 28 percent of the Hispanics, 23 percent of the African Americans, and only 9 percent of the whites. On average, while there were no significant differences by age or race/ethnicity status, there was a trend for women to have been out of work significantly longer than men before going to the job-placement agency (an average of 6.4 years vs. 3.6 years). Likewise, SCSEP enrollees had also been out of work longer than non-SCSEP enrollees (an average of 7.5 years vs. 2.8 years) before going to the job-placement agency.

Summary

Overall, the prior work careers of the part-timers and unemployed elders were quite similar on all dimensions. All but three of the part-timers and all of the unemployed elders had sizable amounts of prior work experience, a fact also noted in other discussions of elder workers regardless of gender (see, for example, Kuriansky and Porter forthcoming; Kronick and Alexander 1993; Ruhm 1990b; Meier 1988). Elders in both groups had experienced a few periods of unemployment across their work lives, the longest of which had lasted about five years, on average. The majority of respondents had left their career job in the late 1970s. Unfortunately, our data does not tell us whether these older workers had sought jobs in the roughly ten-year period since ending their career jobs, or, if they had, what the outcome was. If they had not sought work, whether worker discouragement was a factor is unfortunately unknown.

Regarding their longest or career job, close to a third of the currently unemployed and part-time elders had worked in service positions. About half from each group had worked in clerical, sales, or other office positions, and between 14 to 18 percent from each had worked in professional, technical, or managerial positions. Regardless of job category, these had been full-time jobs, of between 15 and 20 years' duration. Of those reporting specific reasons for leaving their career job, about one-fifth from each group reported leaving their career job involuntarily. About the same number of part-timers, but somewhat fewer of the unemployed, left because they retired or began drawing a pension. About one-tenth of each group cited either poor health or moving as primary. On average, the unemployed and part-time elders had been out of work between four and five years before coming to the placement agency.

As in chapter 4, part 4, there were again significantly more differences among the part-timers than between the part-time and unemployed elders. SCSEP enrollees had experienced significantly more periods of unemployment than non-SCSEP enrollees. Both SCSEP enrollees and women also experienced periods of unemployment of longer duration than either non-SCSEP enrollees or men.

The longest position for all part-timers had been full-time, regardless of their age, gender, race/ethnicity, or SCSEP status. This job had been held about 20 years, except for those elders who were less than 60 years of age or were Hispanic, in which cases it had been held somewhat fewer years. Average hourly earnings were between $5 and $8, with women and SCSEP enrollees earning at the lower end of the range. Hispanics were more likely than whites or African Americans to have left this position involuntarily. Poor health was a factor for relatively few.

Chapter Six
Job-Placement Services and the Older Worker

The comparison of part-time and unemployed interviewees continues in the first section of this chapter, followed by a comparison of their reasons for applying to the job-placement program. The third section examines within-group comparisons of the part-time interviewees.

This chapter addresses the following central questions: (1) How did the previous careers of the unemployed and part-timers mesh with both the kinds of jobs they wished from the placement agency and the kinds of jobs they actually received? and (2) What were the most important reasons participants gave for wanting a job from the placement agency at the time of application?

The Experience of Job Placement for Part-Time and Unemployed Older Workers

Similar to findings comparing part-time and unemployed elders in chapters 4 and 5, the majority of comparisons in this chapter also revealed no significant differences between these two groups of older adults.

About 75 percent of the part-time and unemployed interviewees reported that they wanted either clerical and/or sales or service positions at the time they first applied to the job-placement agency. Around three-quarters from each group were also specifically seeking a part-time job. Thus, the majority of the part-time and unemployed elders in this study reported seeking a part-time job *voluntarily*—because they said they wanted part-time work, not because only part-time work was available or that they could not work more hours because of slack economic conditions.

While the percentage of part-timers in all age categories who work part-time involuntarily has increased significantly in the past twenty-five years (Saltford and Snider 1994; Blank 1990, 1994; Callaghan and Hartmann 1991; Golden 1992), this is balanced by the fact that "over three-fourths of all women part-timers and over half of all men part-timers were working part-time by their own choice in 1987" (Blank 1990), a trend which has continued into the 1990s. Federal labor-force statistics between 1969 and 1993 revealed that even though annual increases in involuntary part-time work were 5.2 percent compared to 2 percent in voluntary part-time work, about 70 percent of all part-time workers were working part-time voluntarily (Saltford and Snider 1994).

According to the literature, post-career jobs commonly penalize elder workers, typically representing a step down in status and pay (Golden 1992; Doeringer 1990b; Burkhauser and Quinn 1989; Herz and Rones 1989; Jondrow, Brechling, and Marcus 1987; Kahne 1985). For our participants, if career continuity is measured by the degree to which the longest jobs held by the elders—their career job as described in chapter 5—are similar in terms of occupational category to the placement jobs they actually received, then the majority of elders did not experience downgrading in occupational status in their placement jobs. This agrees with a finding which Anderson, Burkhauser, and Slotsve (1992) also found for men, using data from the 1970s and 1980s from the Panel Study of Income Dynamics. Across occupational categories, postretirement jobs tended to be in the same occupational category as career jobs. However, those elders in our study—14 percent of the unemployed and 18 percent of the part-timers—who had been in professional, technical, and administrative career jobs, did experience clear occupational downgrading.

At the same time, placement jobs did represent a generalized downgrading in terms of hourly wages for all of the elder workers: the average hourly wage at their career job for all unemployed and part-time elders was between $6.00 and $7.00 an hour, in jobs they vacated in the late 1970s. The starting hourly wage at the placement jobs in 1987–88 was an average of $3.97 for the unemployed elders and $4.14 for the part-timers. Our findings about wage downgrading are generally consistent with those in the literature (Golden 1992; Doeringer 1990b; and Iams 1987). However, while Anderson, Burkhauser, and Slotsve (1992) found some drop in postretirement income, there was more variance in outcome than expected, with some men in lower-wage career jobs actually receiving higher wages in their postretirement jobs.

It is also instructive to examine to what extent the placement jobs part-time and unemployed elders actually received matched the jobs they indicated that they wanted at the time they applied to the placement agency. Such an analysis, comparing the desired job with the actual job received, revealed the following: almost 80 percent of the part-timers and 85 percent of the unemployed who wished a sales or clerical position at the time of application actually received such a position. A similarly high percentage of those wishing service positions—83 percent (39 of 47) of the part-timers and 86 percent (24 of 28) of the unemployed—were also placed in such positions. However, those wishing a professional, technical, or managerial position were less successfully matched: only two of five of the part-timers and one of four of the unemployed actually received such positions.

Thus, even though downgrading occurred in occupational status for some elders and in pay for all elders—most respondents seemed to have a realistic picture of what placement agencies could provide and by and large, got the kinds of positions they reported they were looking for at the time of agency application.

Reasons for Applying to the Job Placement Program

As presented in Table 4, all interviewees were asked to rate how important each of a series of possible reasons for applying to the job-placement agency had been for them at the time of initial application. Two observations are immediately obvious. First there were no significant differences in the mean score ratings on any of the items for part-time and unemployed elders. Second, the rank ordering of the first six items was mostly identical for both groups. Focusing on the first four, "wanting to keep busy," "wanting to work part-time," "needing the money," and "wanting to work close to home," it should first be noted that both groups of elders clearly expressed a desire to work part-time. Two of the other responses were consistent with comments by agency personnel, who consistently indicated that "keeping busy" and "needing the money" were the key issues for their clients. Agency personnel further noted that for many of the

Table 4 Comparison of Reasons for Initial Application to Job-Placement Agency by Unemployed and Part-Time Interviewees

Reason	Unemployed		Part-Timers	
	Mean	Rank	Mean	Rank
Wanted to Keep Busy	3.44	(1)	3.61	(1)
Wanted to Work Part-Time	3.66	(2)	3.51	(2)
Needed Money	3.32	(3)	3.30	(3)
Wanted to Work Close to Home	3.18	(4)	3.24	(4)
Wanted to Help Others	3.15	(5)	3.17	(5)
Wanted to Avoid Loneliness	2.59	(6)	2.61	(6)
Wanted to Work in Something Different	2.54	(7)	2.61	(6)
Wanted Training	2.22	(8)	2.39	(7)
Wanted to Fulfill a Dream	1.91	(9)	1.81	(8)
Pressure from Others	1.51	(10)	1.66	(9)

Score range: 1–4: where 1 = not at all important; 2 = not very important; 3 = somewhat important; and 4 = very important

elders, part-time work was an absolute necessity for economic survival, often resulting in a desperate response—"I'll take anything"—on the part of some elders.

While economic necessity was clearly of great importance to these elder workers, the fact that "wanting to keep busy" was in fact the highest-rated item for part-timers and the second-highest-rated item for the unemployeds should not be overlooked. Blank (1990), in her examination of part-time work for men and women between the ages of 20 and 65 years, conceded that most part-time workers earn lower wages than equally skilled full-time workers and are unambiguously less likely to receive fringe benefits. At the same time she also pointed out that for those part-timers who were working part-time voluntarily, *nonwage* aspects of the decision to work part-time must also be considered in making a final judgment about whether part-time jobs are "good" or "bad" jobs.

Looking at our respondents' reasons for initial application to their job-placement agency, some of the nonwage aspects of these positions, such as the opportunity "to keep busy," a strong desire to work part-time, geographical proximity to their homes, and "wanting to help others" were also important. In fact, for our respondents, keeping busy and active and "wanting to work part-time" were somewhat stronger preferences than "needing the money."

Wanting to "work in something different" and "wanting training" were low priorities for the majority of both part-time and unemployed elders. These responses also coincided with impressions from agency personnel, who, on the whole, indicated that these elder workers were not on a career track—that the majority were interested in working in jobs similar to those they had had in their career job, and were, quite simply, "grateful for the work." This view also corresponds to Sterns and Miklos's (1995) suggestion that older workers may have a different perspective on work than younger workers, tending to have more realistic expectations about the kinds of jobs they are likely to get.

At the same time, these elders fully recognized that they were downwardly mobile in terms of pay. As a staff person from the private, nonprofit agency said: "They are grateful for someone courageous enough to hire them—to give them a chance." The few exceptions to this grateful response were brought out in discussions with the Delaware County key informants, who described special difficulties in getting some highly skilled men, who had been accustomed to $22 per hour as sheet-metal workers, to accept the considerably lower wages that the generally less-skilled placement positions could provide. Although there was little likelihood of these workers being recalled to their old jobs, one staff member said poignantly that: "these men keep thinking they'll be called back to the shipyard." Informants from this same agency indicated that in general, men expected more of the placement positions than women, undoubtedly related to the fact that this agency did place some more highly skilled, male, middle-income elders through its Job Bank program.

About 80 percent of the part-timers were still working in the agency job at the time of their interview and had been doing so for around two years. The roughly 20 percent who were no longer in the agency job, but working elsewhere part-time, had left the agency job rather quickly, after about 4.7 months, significantly sooner than the unemployed, who remained in the agency job about 14.6 months on average.

Reasons for leaving the agency job were significantly different for the two groups. Dissatisfaction with the placement job was cited about twice as often for the part-timers (30 percent) than for the unemployed elders (13 percent). While about one-quarter of the unemployed cited health reasons, less than 5 percent of the part-timers did. This is consistent with findings about differences in perceived health status between the two groups, reported in chapter 4, where unemployed elders reported more limitations in the kind of work they could do, more worry about their physical health, and as having somewhat less energy than the part-timers. Likewise, about twice the number of unemployed elders (10 percent) than part-timers (4 percent) simply wanted to work even less. On the other hand, about one-fifth of the part-timers left to take another job, compared to less than 5 percent of the unemployed elders.

The majority of unemployed and part-time elders left their placement job on their own initiative. While part-timers and unemployed elders were seeking similar types of jobs—largely in sales and/or clerical, and service work—significantly fewer of the unemployed (55 percent vs. 71 percent) got the job they had in mind when they applied to the agency. This frustration, coupled with more expressed concerns about their physical health and somewhat lower energy levels, were all undoubtedly influential in varying degrees in their decision to leave the placement job.

Within-Group Comparisons of the Part-Timers
As presented in chapters 4 and 5, there were more within-group (e.g., by age, gender, race/ethnicity, SCSEP status) than between-group differences between the part-timers and unemployed elders. While there were no significant differences by age or gender, significantly more Hispanics (100 percent) and African Americans (83 percent) than whites (65 percent) and more SCSEP workers (88 percent) than non-SCSEP workers (67 percent) were still in the placement job at the time of the interview, with no significant differences among any of the four subgroups in terms of their length of time in the placement job.

In terms of their desired position at the time of application, age was again not significant, but differences by gender, minority, and SCSEP status were. Significantly more males than females (8 per-

cent vs. less than 1 percent) desired professional, technical, or managerial positions, while more females desired clerical and sales positions (49 percent vs. 41 percent). As before, significantly more whites
than African Americans or Hispanics (55 percent vs. 44 percent vs.
39 percent) desired clerical and sales positions. Likewise, significantly
more non-SCSEP enrollees than SCSEP enrollees desired professional positions.

In terms of the actual positions secured by the placement agencies, the patterns were again similar. Significantly more females than
males secured clerical and sales positions (46 percent vs. 33 percent), as did whites (55 percent) compared to African Americans
(35 percent) and Hispanics (31 percent). Likewise, similar trends
differentiated non-SCSEP workers from SCSEP enrollees. Finally
there were no significant variations by age, minority status, gender
or SCSEP status in terms of whether or not the part-timers secured
the job they wished to receive from the placement agency.

An examination of the four highest-ranked reasons for the elders' initial application to the job-placement agency revealed significant differences only in terms of ranking the item wanting to
"keep busy," with SCSEP enrollees rating this item somewhat higher
than non-SCSEP workers. Regarding the desire to "work part-time,"
there were no differences by gender or SCSEP status. However, there
were significant differences by age—with those elders in the youngest age group (55–59 years) rating this item as less important to
them—and by minority status, with Hispanics also rating this item
as somewhat less important than either African American or white
respondents. In terms of the importance of needing the money, while
there were no significant differences by age or gender, Hispanics
rated this as more important than did either African Americans or
whites; SCSEP workers did the same. Finally in terms of the importance of working "close to home," the only significant differences
were by SCSEP status, with SCSEP workers as a group rating this
item higher than non-SCSEP workers.

Focusing on the Hispanic elderly more specifically, according
to the agency key informant, while both male and female Hispanic
elders worked primarily because of economic necessity, the perceived
need for income differed between men and women. As she indicated, "when a Hispanic man stops working, his pride is at stake."

The older male Hispanic workers want to work to prove that they "are man enough to bring home the money." According to this informant, this element of pride in working and feelings of shame about not working were not expressed by the female Hispanic workers. As a consequence, many Hispanic male elders "will accept practically anything, even sweeping the streets, as long as they are earning money," which was not true for the Hispanic female elders.

Summary

As in chapters 4 and 5, the majority of results in chapter 6 revealed no significant differences between the part-time and unemployed elderly in terms of the degree to which their placement jobs were continuous with their career jobs. By and large, there was career continuity for the majority of elders—both part-time and unemployed—particularly if their career jobs had been in clerical and/or sales or service positions. Those elders who had been in professional, technical, or managerial positions earlier experienced the greatest downward mobility in terms of job-classification status in the agency-placement jobs. Salary decrements were experienced by the majority of elder workers in their placement jobs, regardless of career job classification. Such declines are the norm for older workers who move from full-time positions, where they may have had considerable seniority, to part-time jobs in new work sites, where they are "new hires" (Golden 1992; Burkhauser and Quinn 1989; Morrison 1986).

In spite of downgrading in terms of salary for the majority of elders, and occupational downgrading for some of the elders—especially those who had been in professional, technical, or administrative positions as younger workers—elder workers, by and large, received the kinds of jobs they wanted when they applied to the placement agencies. The two most important reasons cited for initial application to their placement agencies was the same for both the unemployeds and those working part-time—"their desire for a part-time job" and wanting to "keep busy." "Working close to home" and "helping others" were also other nonwage preferences.

For the majority of these elders, part-time employment provided an essential supplement to an already marginal economic existence. Judging from the low household incomes most elders had, the extra earnings from part-time employment were absolutely essential to make ends meet. Likewise the value of "keeping busy"—a highly ranked reason for their working part-time—should not be overlooked in assessing the overall value of part-time positions for these elders. These two reasons also coincide with the first two functions of work, described by Friedmann and Havighurst in 1954—income or financial return and work as a regulator of life activity, providing order and routine to life.

The response of these elders to part-time employment was therefore quite pragmatic and realistic. By and large, they were not seeking new challenges in terms of additional training or the opportunity to try their hand at something different, although such opportunities were favorably responded to, if they occurred. The majority of elders also indicated that "working close to home" was a high priority. Although this response was in part related to realistic fears about the physical safety of travel beyond one's neighborhood, it was at the same time a pragmatic response, related to considerations about time and costs.

The majority of the part-timers were still in the placement agency job at the time of their interview. Also significantly more of the part-timers than the unemployed elders reported that they had, in fact, *gotten* the job they had in mind when they first came to the agency. Other differences emerged when the reasons for leaving the placement job were compared for the minority of part-timers and the group of unemployed elders who had vacated their agency position by the time of their interviews. Consistent with the results in chapter 4 concerning differences in perceived health status between the part-time and unemployed elders, significantly more of the unemployed reported that they left the placement job either because of poor health or because they wanted to work less. On the other hand, those part-timers who left the placement job and were now working part-time elsewhere reported more often than the unemployed did leaving the placement position because they took a job elsewhere or because they were dissatisfied with the placement job.

When differences by age, gender, minority, and SCSEP status were examined for the part-timers, differences by age emerged infrequently and the rest of the differences were in the expected direction. For example, in terms of gender differences, women were more likely to desire and get clerical and sales or service positions than men. Likewise, Hispanics and SCSEP workers, both of whom were poorer overall than other groups of workers, rated "needing the money" as more important to them in seeking a part-time job than did either African Americans, whites, or non-SCSEP workers.

Chapter Seven
The Structural Characteristics of Part-Time Work

This chapter begins by describing the general structural characteristics of the elder workers' (N=164) part-time positions at the time of their interviews, including the kinds of jobs they held, how long they had held them, the size of the organizations where they were placed, the number of hours and days worked per week, the amount of time spent commuting, and hourly wages. Next, we consider the regularity of their schedules, followed by an analysis of their fringe benefits. Any variations by age, gender, minority, and SCSEP status are discussed in each section.

As noted in chapter 2, some of the structural characteristics of a job, including wages, fringe benefits, and schedule regularity are among the factors commonly used to assess overall job quality.

General Structural Characteristics of the Part-Time Positions

The majority of elder part-time employees were working in clerical and/or sales and service positions. More specifically, 41 percent (67) were employed as clerks, 23 percent as aides (38), 12 percent (19) as counselors, 10 percent (17) as security and maintenance workers, 6 percent (10) as drivers, and 8 percent (13) in miscellaneous kinds of positions. These positions were typically located in day-care and senior centers, in people's homes, and in a range of small (less than 100 employees) nonprofit and for-profit organizations. Although there were no significant differences by age, there were significant variations by gender, race/ethnicity, and SCSEP status. More specifically, males were more likely than females to be security and maintenance workers (23.5 percent vs. 4 percent of women) or drivers (14 percent vs. 2 percent of women), while women were more likely to be clerks (45 percent vs. 33 percent of men) or aides (30 percent vs. 10 percent of men). Slightly over 10 percent of men and women were counselors.

The majority of whites were clerks (62.5 percent). While almost one-third of the Hispanics were clerks, 28 percent were security or maintenance workers, 22 percent were aides, and 12.5 percent were counselors. About one-third of the African Americans were aides, 28 percent were clerks, 15 percent were counselors, and almost 10 percent were security and maintenance workers. Small percentages of African Americans (7 percent) and whites (9 percent) and none of the Hispanics were drivers. About 10 percent of both SCSEP and non-SCSEP workers were security and maintenance workers, and about 40 percent of each were clerks. Significantly more of the SCSEP workers were counselors (19 percent vs. 6 percent of non-SCSEP workers) and significantly fewer of them were drivers (2 percent vs. 11 percent).

About 80 percent of the part-timers had gotten their jobs through the job-placement agency, with significantly more of the Hispanics (97 percent) than African Americans (80 percent) and whites (68 percent), and SCSEP (86 percent) than non-SCSEP workers (69 percent) having done so. As a group, the elder workers had held these jobs for about two years, with SCSEP workers having held their jobs significantly longer than non-SCSEP workers.

Part-time elder employees worked, on average, 20 hours a week, with no significant variations by age, gender, race/ethnicity, or SCSEP status. The number of hours worked generally conformed to the national average for all part-time workers during the mid-1980s (9 to 5 1986). The elders worked, on average, four days per week, with Hispanics and African Americans more likely to work more days than whites.

Almost half (44.8 percent) used public transportation, while close to one-third (31 percent) used their own car, and 15 percent walked to work. Negligible numbers used someone else's car, a company vehicle, or other forms of transportation. Two times as many males as females drove themselves to work (56 percent vs. 28 percent), while women were much more likely to use public transportation (56 percent vs. 24 percent). African Americans (64 percent) were much more likely to use public transportation than either Hispanics (42 percent) or whites (25 percent). Less than one-quarter of all elders walked to work. Finally, SCSEP workers (56 percent) were almost twice as likely to use public transportation as non-SCSEP workers (29 percent).

The average time spent commuting was 48 minutes round-trip, with variations only by gender. Women spent, on average, 11 minutes longer commuting than men. These commuting times were somewhat shorter than national averages for workers across the life span during the 1980s (Wright 1990). At that time, the average travel time for those commuting by car was 45 minutes round-trip and over an hour (72.4 minutes) for those commuting by bus (Pisarski 1987).

While the actual number of hours worked each day varied among the part-timers, let's imagine that an elder employee worked a four-day week, five hours a day, and commuted close to an hour round-trip. If the elder worker used public transportation, which close to half did, additional time might be added for walking to and from the bus or trolley. This could begin to feel like a full-time work week. We are reminded of one elder female part-time worker, who, when asked how long she had been working part-time, seemed puzzled by the question. She said that she worked full-time. When the interviewer told her that she had indicated that she worked 20 hours a week, the elder worker responded that because she went to work every day and was gone for most of the day, it "felt like a full-time job," a feeling easy to imagine.

In response to the question "How much time would you be willing to spend traveling to and from work?, elder workers as a whole indicated they would be willing to spend close to an hour (59 minutes), or roughly 10 to 15 minutes more than they were spending now. Once again, the only significant variation was by gender, with women expressing a willingness to spend an average of about an hour traveling, versus about 50 minutes for men.

Finally, the mean hourly wage for all part-time elder workers was $4.78 an hour, with a median of $4.00 and a standard deviation of $1.75. This hourly wage was somewhat lower than the median hourly wage reported for all part-timers in 1985 of $4.17 (Plewes 1988) and in 1987 of $4.42 (Kahne 1992). Although elder males in our study earned a higher average salary than did elder females ($5.11

vs. $4.62), these results were not statistically significant, nor were the results comparing salaries by different age groups.

However, there were significant salary differences by SCSEP status and by minority status. In terms of the former, non-SCSEP workers earned significantly more an hour than SCSEP employees, with an average of $5.63 compared to an average of $4.21 an hour for SCSEP enrollees. Recall from chapter 3 that all SCSEP enrollees are paid at minimum-wage rates—either the existing federal or state minimum wage, whichever is higher. Further, white elders earned significantly more an hour ($5.45) than Hispanics ($3.98) or African Americans ($4.67).

These hourly wages were lower than those reported for all employees working part-time in 1987, reported by Blank (1990). According to Current Population Survey figures in 1987, all female workers between the ages of 18 and 65 years, working part-time, earned an average hourly wage (mean wage) of $8.03 an hour. There were obvious differences among occupational categories, with women in professional, managerial, and technical positions earning an average of $11.32 an hour, while those in sales, clerical, and service positions, earned the following per hour, respectively: $7.73, $7.70, and $6.27.

Using the same Current Population Survey data, Blank reported that the average (mean) hourly rate for all males working part-time in 1987 was $12.46, with a high of $19.29 for those males working part-time in professional, technical, and managerial positions; $13.34 an hour for those in sales; $8.60 for those in clerical positions; and $8.78 an hour for those in service positions. Elder males in our study earned an average of $5.11 an hour. Thus both elder female and male part-time workers in this study earned a lower mean hourly wage than all part-time workers of both genders in 1987, both overall and when examined by occupational category. It should be noted, however, that the upper age limit used by Blank was 65; about two-thirds of our part-time respondents were 65 and over.

When gender, minority status, age, and SCSEP status were used as independent variables in a multiple regression analysis, with hourly wages as the dependent variable, SCSEP status and minority status proved to be significant factors, together accounting for 19 percent of the variance in hourly earnings. In other words, controlling for age, gender, and minority status, non-SCSEP enrollees and whites earned more per hour than SCSEP enrollees and Hispanics and African Americans. Based on regression analysis, then, both SCSEP status and race/ethnicity status emerged as significant predictors of hourly wages, not gender or age.

Schedule Regularity

While chapter 8 will examine the flip side of the regularity issue—schedule flexibility—one of the key characteristics of contingent work arrangements is the *unpredictability* of hours at work. With contingent work arrangements, hours are routinely determined at the whim of the employer, without consultation with the employee (Polivka and Nardone 1989).

Over 80 percent of all part-time elder workers in this study worked the same days and hours each week and described their work as being regular, steady work, rather than seasonal or other forms of unsteady employment. The only significant differences emerged around the following question: "Do you work the same hours each week?," with workers in the 70–74-year age range reporting significantly less regularity of hours than other age categories. Even in this case, however, 65 percent of those 70–74 years old reported regularity of hours. Likewise, white elders reported significantly less regularity in hours than Hispanics or African Americans. Here too, though, about three-quarters of the whites reported regularity of hours. Finally, even though SCSEP workers reported significantly more regularity in hours than non-SCSEP workers, again, over 75 percent of the non-SCSEP workers reported regularity in hours. While we did not directly ask how secure they perceived their jobs to be, the fact that the part-time elders in our study overwhelmingly viewed their jobs as regular, nonseasonal jobs, with schedule regularity, provides at least some indirect support for perceived job security, a component of job quality in Jencks, Perman, and Rainwater's (1988) and Karasek and Theorell's (1990) schemes.

One additional aspect of employment related to schedule regularity is the issue of overtime work. Overall, about one-third of the elder workers reported working overtime at some point on their jobs, with no significant differences by race, minority, or SCSEP status. However, more workers in the 60–64-year and 70–74-year age ranges reported having the opportunity to work overtime than elders in the other three age categories. Whether working overtime was voluntary or not was not asked. We did ask, however, about financial compensation for overtime work.

According to a study by Carr (1986), about 90 percent of workers reporting working overtime in 1985 were paid "time and one-half." Further, more than half of those reporting some work at overtime rates were in the skilled trades—precision production, craft, and repair group—followed closely by those who were operators, fabricators, and laborers. None of our respondents had such positions. Likewise, it was men in the 25- to 34-year-old age group who were most likely to put in extra hours at overtime rates, with progressive declines for both genders by age. Whites were also somewhat more likely to work at overtime rates than African Americans or Hispanics (Carr 1986).

Not surprisingly, then, in examining how the elders in this study who worked overtime were compensated, 44 percent received no compensation; about one-third received compensation at their regular hourly rate; about 15 percent received compensatory time off; about 7 percent received "time-and-one-half"; and about 3 percent received some combination of the above. According to Olmsted and Smith (1989):

Overtime becomes a particularly sensitive issue for part-timers when management's expectation is that part-time employees will regularly work overtime at straight pay. When this is a "hidden agenda," it undermines the working relationship of part-timers and their employer. (p. 75)

According to these authors, then, those elders in our sample who worked overtime—the majority of whom received no compensation or straight hourly pay—were definitely being exploited.

Fringe Benefits

As discussed in chapter 2, one of the critical variables separating so-called contingent work from other forms of work (Tilly 1996; Blank 1997; Parker 1994; duRivage 1992; Belous 1989b), so-called "good" part-time work from "bad" part-time work (Blank 1990)—New Concept from Old Concept part-time work (Kahne 1986), or retention part-time work from secondary part-time work (Tilly 1996, 1992a)—is the payment of fringe benefits to part-time workers, usually on a prorated basis. Looking at health insurance and pension coverage as two of the most important benefits to workers, Tilly (1990, p. 10) concluded:

Fringe benefits are not characteristic of part-time employment. Approximately 22 percent of part-time workers receive health insurance as a benefit, compared to 78 percent of full-time workers (Rebitzer and Taylor 1988). . . . Similarly, only 26 percent of part-timers have employer-supplied pension coverage, whereas nearly 60 percent of full-timers enjoy such coverage (Rebitzer and Taylor 1988). Part-time workers are also about 20 percent less likely than those on full-time schedules to receive any sick leave or paid vacation (Ichniowski and Preston 1985).

Using the 1987 Current Population Survey data, Blank's (1990) conclusions were somewhat more conservative, but in the same direction. To quote: "Among all workers, only 14 to 18 percent of part-time employees are included in a pension plan, while 50 to 58 percent of full-time employees are covered by a plan" (p. 131). While health-insurance coverage was more common than pension coverage, there were distinct variations by gender and occupation. Of all female heads-of-households, 26 percent of part-time versus 74 percent of full-time working women received health coverage in 1987. In the same year, for men, of those working part-time, 37 percent compared to 79 percent of those working full-time received coverage. Whether part- or full-time, service workers were least likely to receive health coverage or pensions while managerial and professional workers were most likely to receive them. Overall then: "In general, across all occupations part-time workers are one-third to one-half as likely as full-time workers to receive benefits" (Blank 1990, 131). Such disparities in benefit coverage continued to be reported in the 1990s (Saltford and Snider 1994; duRivage 1992; and General Accounting Office 1991).

How did the elder workers in this study fare in terms of fringe benefits and were there any variations by age, gender, minority, or SCSEP status? Table 5 summarizes the data on fringe benefits for all part-time elder workers, using the Part-Time Fringe Benefits Index.

This index, developed by Quinn and Staines (1979), measures the range and quantity of benefits received. The alpha reliability coefficient for the Part-Time Fringe Benefits Index was 0.77. It contains the identical set of items found in the Full-Time Fringe Benefits Index, discussed in chapter 13, and is also scored on the same two-point scale, where 1 = the receipt of the benefit and 0 = the nonreceipt of the benefit.

Examining Table 5 in more detail, the most obvious conclusion is that the overall level of fringe benefits was quite low for our respondents, although there was variation among some of the items. For example, while only about one-tenth of the elder workers received health coverage, clearly less than the figure cited above by Blank for either part-time male or female workers, far more received sick leave with full pay (47 percent). Almost 20 percent received free or discounted meals, close to 40 percent received some kind of additional training or education; 57 percent received paid holidays, and 58 percent received paid vacations. A negligible percent—4 percent—received pension coverage.

In general, then, the elders were more likely to receive benefits which were less costly to employers, such as sick leave, with full or part pay; and paid vacations and holidays; and least likely to receive the more costly benefits such as health insurance and pension coverage.

When the overall index score was examined for age, gender, minority, and SCSEP status variations, there were no significant variations by gender. However, the youngest and oldest age groups were more likely to have a higher index score, as were Hispanics, and SCSEP workers. In terms of the age differential, some of the more highly skilled males were undoubtedly in both of these categories, which could account for the difference.

In terms of the minority and SCSEP status differentials, discussions with agency personnel were enlightening. Two out of three of the SCSEP programs required some benefit coverage. In addition to the annual physical and Workmen's Compensation, which are required by SCSEP programs nationwide, two of the study SCSEP programs required some paid sick leave, paid vacation time, and paid holidays. The third SCSEP program did not require these latter three benefits, however, accounting for the slightly lower overall benefit level for the SCSEP workers. Likewise, the fact that Hispanics proportionately received more benefits was because all but one of the Hispanic elderly were SCSEP workers, in an SCSEP program

Table 5 Fringe Benefits Received by Part-Time Employed Survey Respondents (Part-Time Fringe Benefits Index)

		Receipt				
		Yes		No		
Fringe Benefit		No.	%	No.	%	Mean[a]
1. Medical, surgical, or hospital insurance covering any illness or injury occurring while *off* the job		16	10.1	143	89.9	0.10
2. Sick leave with full pay		76	46.9	86	53.1	0.47
3. Sick leave with part pay		14	9.5	133	90.5	0.09
4. Dental benefits		6	3.8	150	96.2	0.04
5. Eyeglass or eyecare benefits		5	3.2	152	96.8	0.03
6. Life insurance that would cover a death occurring for reasons *not* connected with your job		7	4.5	150	95.5	0.04
7. Pension/annuity program		7	4.4	153	95.6	0.04
8. Profit sharing		2	1.3	153	98.7	0.01
9. Thrift or savings program		4	2.6	150	97.4	0.03
10. Free or discounted meals		31	19.6	127	80.4	0.20
11. Free or discounted merchandise		10	6.5	145	93.5	0.06
12. Stock options		0	0.0	154	100.0	0.00
13. Legal aid or services		9	5.8	146	94.2	0.06
14. Training or education program you can take to improve your skills		62	39.2	96	60.8	0.39
15. Work clothing allowance		9	5.8	146	94.2	0.06
16. Paid vacation		94	58.0	68	42.0	0.58
17. Paid holidays		92	57.1	69	42.9	0.57
Index Score[a]						0.18

Index SD = 0.19, alpha = 0.77
[a]Mean item and index score range 0–1, where a higher score indicates greater frequency of receipt of fringe benefits.

which required certain benefits of its placement sites, including paid sick leave, paid vacation time, and paid holidays.

How did elder workers feel about fringe benefits? In general, they thought that providing more fringe benefits was a good idea but had no real expectation that such would be offered. Further information about the kinds of "wish lists" they had for the most desirable types of benefits are addressed in chapter 9. How did agency personnel feel about the fringe-benefit question? According to key informants from the private nonprofit agency, employers did not expect to give health benefits to older employees because they assumed they had medical benefits through Medicare. At the same time these informants were quite surprised to learn from discussions with the principal investigators that most employers they used did not routinely provide paid holidays, paid sick leave, and some paid vacation days, benefits which they felt strongly should be—and assumed, in some instances—were being provided.

Overall, while key informants from the four agencies felt that more fringe benefits should be provided, they did not regard this issue as one of their high priorities to be negotiated with employers and potential employers. The overall sense was that employer response would be negative and they were resigned to this response.

Summary

The majority of elder part-time workers were working at the job the placement agency had gotten for them, where they had been for around two years. On average, they worked 20 hours a week, four days a week, and spent about three-quarters of an hour commuting. The kinds of positions they held were mostly as clerks, aides, counselors, security and maintenance workers, and drivers, in that order. There were distinct gender differences, with males more likely to be security and maintenance workers or drivers than females; female workers, on the other hand, were more likely to be clerks or aides than males. There was also variation by minority status: the majority of white elders were clerks; the majority of Hispanic elders, either clerks, security workers, or aides; and the majority of African Americans, either aides or clerks. Over three-quarters of these positions were seen as regular, steady positions, rather than seasonal or other kinds of unsteady employment.

While above the minimum wage for 1985, the median hourly wage for study elders was somewhat lower than median hourly wages reported for all part-time workers in 1985, and moderately lower than mean hourly wages for all part-time workers, based on 1987 Current Population Survey figures. Overall receipt of fringe benefits was quite low for the elders, though SCSEP and Hispanic workers were more likely to receive some benefits than non-SCSEP and white and African American workers. Thus, if wages and benefits are the *only* indicators of job quality used, the part-time positions of study respondents would have to be considered "bad" part-time jobs. If wages and benefits are considered to be *among* rather than the *only* indicators of job quality, then these part-time jobs would receive two checks each under the "bad" part-time job column. On the other hand, the fact that these part-time jobs were also perceived to be steady, nonseasonal jobs and jobs with predictable working hours earns two checks under the "good" part-time job column.

Chapter Eight
The Functional Characteristics of Part-Time Work

This chapter presents data about what we have termed the "perceived functions" of part-time work for the 164 elders still employed part-time when interviewed. By functions, we have included issues of skills acquisition and utilization, interaction with others in the workplace, and the extent to which elder workers felt they had control over altering their work schedules. Specifically, findings are presented which reflect the extent to which older workers were able to:

1. Use existing skills or acquire new expertise in their jobs
2. Interact on the job with co-workers generally and other part-timers in particular
3. Associate at work with younger people as well as other employees their own age
4. Exercise some control over their work schedules.

The ability to use existing skills and/or acquire new ones and to exercise some control over work schedules are two indicators among those commonly used to assess overall job quality, according to Karasek and Theorell (1990); Rosenthal (1989); and Jencks, Perman, and Rainwater (1988). These are also job characteristics associated with "good" rather than "bad" part-time jobs.

Utilization of Existing Skills and Acquisition of New Skills

Part-time workers were asked about the extent to which they felt they were able to either use existing skills they brought to the placement or acquire new expertise in their part-time jobs. About 75 percent felt they were able to apply their existing expertise to the placement job; about two-thirds reported acquiring new skills in their placements. Females were significantly more likely than males to use existing skills and Hispanics were significantly less likely than African Americans or whites to do the same. There were no statistical differences by age. Unfortunately, we did not ask respondents to elaborate on the nature of these new or existing skills. However, some elders reported this information spontaneously, so we have included some of this anecdotal evidence.

For example, one 73-year-old Hispanic woman's placement job was to teach other elders how to sew. She had not realized before going to Project Ayuda that she could make money teaching others to do something she had done all of her life. A 66-year-old African American male came to the placement job with previous training to do a range of semiskilled jobs. However, his placement position as a dispatcher and security person, responsible for monitoring the movement of Wells Fargo trucks, had enabled him to learn to type and to use a computer. A 78-year-old white female, placed as a telephone receptionist, had learned how to work a complicated photocopying machine. While she had mastered this new skill, at the same time she also complained:

"The agency should spend more time helping them [new staff] in training. We need more training over time, not all at the beginning." She did not think that the agency should assume that you know how to work equipment [photocopiers]. However, she pointed out that she had learned to speak up and ask for help. "Now I'm very efficient at it (using photocopiers)."

Whereas Hispanics were less likely to report applying existing skills to their placement jobs, they were significantly more likely to report having acquired new skills in their job placements. Persons placed in SCSEP employment were also significantly more likely to report that they had acquired new job skills than those placed in non-SCSEP employment.

Opportunities for Interaction in the Workplace
Respondents were also asked a series of questions concerning the extent to which they were able to interact with others on the job. As

pointed out by Friedmann and Havighurst (1954), developing mean-ingful social relationships is an important function of work. Respon-dents indicated they worked with an average of 11 other workers, of whom almost half were part-timers like themselves. Hispanics and SCSEP workers reported having significantly larger numbers of co-workers with whom to interact. Similarly, Hispanic respondents re-ported working with significantly larger numbers of part-time co-workers compared to their African American and white counterparts. Further, close to two-thirds of the respondents indicated that a good number of their co-workers who were working part-time were also older workers. Opportunities to work with other part-time employ-ees, both younger and older, provided a supportive organizational context and is one important factor that reduces structural margin-ality.

About 80 percent of the respondents indicated that they had a chance to work with younger people on the job; almost 70 percent indicated they worked with people their own age. These opportuni-ties were, however, significantly greater for Hispanics and SCSEP workers than for African American, white, or non-SCSEP workers. There were no significant differences in perceived opportunities for intergenerational workplace interaction by gender, age, minority, or SCSEP status.

Flexibility and Work Schedules

To what extent did these elders perceive that they could exercise some scheduling flexibility in their jobs? More specifically, respon-dents were asked to assess the extent to which they believed their job schedules could be altered. The views of part-timers were remark-ably similar across gender, race, age, and SCSEP categories. Scored on a four-point scale where 1 = "not at all hard," 2 = "not too hard," 3 = "somewhat hard," and 4 = "very hard," aggregate responses of those surveyed clustered around the midpoint or below. Clearly re-spondents believed it was much easier to take time off during the day for personal or family matters than to attempt to alter their work schedules permanently by changing the days that they worked or the hourly requirements.

On average, respondents believed it would be "not at all hard" to "not too hard" to take time off during the day for personal reasons. On the other hand, the mean levels of difficulty associated with changing their work hours and days at work were considerably higher. Nonetheless, respondents reported high levels of satisfaction with the hours and days that they worked. Almost nine of every ten workers were satisfied with the hours that they worked. Those few who were not satisfied typically wished they could work more hours.

Nine out of ten respondents also indicated that the days they worked suited them. Further, these latter data did not reflect the total absence of perceived opportunities to alter their hours or days at work for some elders. For example, a 70-year-old African American woman working as a receptionist enjoyed, in particular, the flexibility of her present employment and felt she got along well with her co-workers and supervisor. The greatest benefit of the job, in her opinion, was the flexibility in that she was able to have her grandchildren with her during work hours. Similarly, a 78-year-old woman working part-time as a communications director with a job-placement agency felt her job suited her way of life. "It is flexible and allows me time for other things," she said. This was also the case for a 77-year-old woman who worked as a friendly visitor for the social service department of a senior center. She worked approximately 20 hours a week but maintained a very flexible schedule in terms of the particular days and the number of hours she worked each day.

Schedule regularity was a mixed blessing for some elders, however. A 75-year-old man working as an elderly victim's advocate with a local organization disliked his "inflexible schedule." A 72-year-old widow, working as a personnel clerk in a large corporation also felt restricted by the requirement that she had to be on the job during the same days and hours each week.

Some job-placement staff viewed placement positions as somewhat flexible in terms of specified days and hours at work. One director pointed out that participants were frequently able to choose which days and hours they would work within the limitations set by the employer. Many of the jobs offered flextime as an option, allowing additional latitude in work schedules. This was said to be the case across a range of available jobs, and as one director put it, "Employees can always refuse to accept the job." According to another agency director, SCSEP jobs which were subsidized were especially flexible for the older worker because their work was free for the employer.

Placement jobs in the private sector tended to be less flexible. However, some agency personnel felt this might change due to the growing interest in part-time jobs by the private sector.

When part-timers assessed the opportunities for transforming their part-time jobs to full-time positions, almost two-thirds of the respondents believed that their current employers would say no to such a request. Even so, one-third of those surveyed believed that they would be able to assume full-time employment if they so wished. While there were no significant differences by gender, minority status, and age, there were significant differences by SCSEP status. SCSEP enrollees were less likely to report the likelihood of converting their part-time jobs to full-time. Because SCSEP jobs were by definition part-time jobs, it was not at all surprising that SCSEP enrollees perceived limited convertibility.

The convertibility of part-time to full-time jobs within the same job setting is an issue for part-time workers of any age, in any kind of job, and in any kind of setting. It is also one which has received limited research attention (Blank 1990). However, Blank (1994), using 14 years of data (1976 to 1989) from the Panel Study of Income Dynamics, reported that at least for younger female workers, part-time work was used primarily either as an alternative to full-time work or to being out of the labor force entirely. Few women used it as a transitional step into full-time employment. While we are not aware of similar studies with older workers, our respondents were undoubtedly realistic appraisers of this important issue for part-time work in general.

Summary
Even though the kinds of jobs part-timers received ranked low in occupational prestige, both the utilization of existing skills and the acquisition of new expertise were still reported by the majority of part-time elder workers. Both of these characteristics are commonly considered as indicators of good job quality and merit one check each under the "good" part-time job column. Females were more likely to have opportunities to use their existing capacities, whereas Hispanics were least likely. On the other hand, Hispanics and SCSEP workers were convinced that they had greater opportunities to acquire new job skills, though we did not specifically ask what these skills were.

Hispanics and SCSEP workers were apparently working in settings which provided more opportunities for co-worker interaction; Hispanic employees in particular were most likely to be working with other part-time employees. A clear majority of the elder part-time workers also reported having opportunities to work with younger persons as well as members of their own age cohort in their placement jobs. According to Friedmann and Havighurst (1954), the opportunity for positive social relationships is an important function of work. Opportunities for intergenerational interaction were greatest for Hispanics and SCSEP workers.

Agency staff maintained that SCSEP-subsidized placements in particular offered workers the greatest degree of work schedule flexibility. According to elder part-time workers, they had faced few barriers in taking time off as needed to attend to personal and family responsibilities. There was less perceived flexibility around altering hourly or daily work schedules permanently, if a worker so wished. Even so, nine out of ten workers reported that they were satisfied with the hours and days that they worked. As another indicator of good job quality, the category of schedule flexibility seems best rated as midway between the "good" part-time job—"bad" part-time job columns.

Similarly, the majority of employees reported that they would be unable to transform their part-time positions to full-time jobs if they made such a request. Conversion to full-time work was believed to be least feasible by Hispanic and SCSEP workers. Although this issue of schedule convertibility (from part- to full-time) has received no formal research attention that we are aware of in the case of older workers, the work which has been done with younger female workers suggests that schedule convertibility, while desired by some, is not a common occurrence.

Chapter Nine
Satisfaction with Part-Time Employment

Did older adults employed in part-time jobs find their work satisfying? To what extent did these individuals express commitment to their workplace responsibilities? Specifically, data are considered which addressed:

1. The degree of overall satisfaction with the job
2. The level of effort expended in performing their jobs
3. The extent to which workplace issues permeated the worker's family life, both positively and negatively
4. The level of enjoyment associated with working with younger workers and other part-time workers their own age
5. Desirable fringe benefits
6. The predictors of job satisfaction

Job Satisfaction and the Older Worker

In order to assess job satisfaction, a shortened and modified version of Quinn and Staines' (1979) nine-item job satisfaction index was used. The index constructed for this study was a six-item forced-choice measure, scored on a four-point scale, where a higher score reflected greater levels of job satisfaction. This index was moderately reliable (alpha = 0.63).

As shown in Table 6, the total index score for the Job Satisfaction Index (JSI) was in the upper quartile, indicating relatively high levels of job satisfaction. Satisfaction was greatest in terms of the physical surroundings in which these elders worked and the capacity of supervisors to encourage positive working relationships among employees. Overall job satisfaction was ranked equally high. The lack of good fringe benefits, also discussed in chapter 7, was the least satisfying aspect of their employment and was rated substantially lower than any other dimension of the job (more will be said about this later).

Satisfaction levels did not differ significantly by age, gender, or SCSEP status. However, white employees were found to be significantly less satisfied with their employment experiences than Hispanic or African American workers. Even so, white respondents still recorded a relatively high level of satisfaction as gauged by the JSI. Hispanic employee-satisfaction levels were the highest of all subgroups of respondents.

Job-placement program directors and staff also spoke of high levels of job satisfaction among older workers. One director estimated that over 90 percent of the older adults, placed in a part-time position, were satisfied with their jobs. He maintained that the few who called to complain were usually dissatisfied with the working conditions or disliked working with younger people. He went on to say that some older workers felt pressured by family members (husbands in particular) who were unhappy that their older relative was no longer at home all the time. Others were pleasantly surprised by how much they enjoyed having the extra income. The most successful placements, according to this director, were those in which workers were employed in positions they specifically requested, which was also one of the ob-

Table 6 Extent of Job Satisfaction among Part-Time Elder Workers (Job Satisfaction Index)

Job Satisfaction Items	Mean[a]
Degree to which worker agrees with each statement (1–4 points):	
1. My fringe benefits are good.	2.0
2. The physical surroundings are pleasant.	3.7
3. I am free from people making conflicting demands on me on the job.	3.4
4. My supervisor is successful in getting people to work together.	3.7
5. The people I work with take a personal interest in me.	3.5
6. All in all, how satisfied would you say you are with your job?	3.7
Index Score	3.3

Index SD = 0.54, alpha = 0.63
[a]Individual item and index score range 1–4, where a higher score indicates greater agreement (satisfaction) with the statement(s).

servations made in chapter 6, and one which distinguished those elders still working part-time from those who were unemployed.

One agency director reported that ingredients for a successful placement included an ideal wage, ideal hours, and an employer who was sensitive to the older person who was returning to the work force. The definitions of ideal wages and ideal hours varied from one elder worker to another. Another director added proximity to home as an important variable figuring in the successful placement, a variable whose importance was also addressed in chapter 7. One director maintained that many workers were willing to accept less than their ideal wage, but that this could ultimately downgrade overall job satisfaction.

Several employment-agency staff suggested that placement success had less to do with the type of work done than one might think. Among some of the "success stories" at one agency were a bank manager who accepted a job as a messenger, and a doctor who has worked as a bellhop in a resort community on the Jersey shore and as a busboy at a restaurant in Philadelphia. Both were very satisfied with their jobs.

Finally, one agency official determined job satisfaction by the retention rate—the length of time the older worker remained on the job. He pointed out that the subsidized positions had a superior retention rate compared to the private-sector positions, perhaps suggesting higher levels of job satisfaction. Furthermore, those agencies that made special efforts to accommodate the needs of the older worker were also those that generally made the most successful placements. Examples of such accommodation included the creation of shared positions and allowing for special arrangements in work scheduling.

According to this same key informant, another factor that contributed to a successful placement in the subsidized jobs was the employer's intention to ultimately hire the individual directly, rather than have him or her remain indefinitely in a subsidized position. While few in number, some of the agencies that had been open to making this type of transition included travel agencies, banks, cultural institutions, and some social service agencies.

Job Effort and Family Life Influences

Overall job quality was also assessed by the reported level of effort expended on the job and the relationship between the elder's work life and life away from the job. A series of questions addressing these aspects of job quality and job satisfaction were asked of elder workers.

Generally speaking, there was considerable agreement among respondent subgroups on these issues. About 90 percent of the elders maintained that they put "some" to "a lot" more effort, beyond what was required, into their jobs. About 70 percent also maintained that on most days, time seemed either "never" or "rarely" to drag for them. Time drag was reported as a rare occurrence across all respondent subgroups.

The application of extra effort on the job was also reported to be relatively common for all subgroups, although Hispanics reported applying significantly less extra effort than their white counterparts. African American workers rated themselves in the mid-range on this variable.

In terms of the relationship between an individual's work and family life, the association was a positive one. Over three-quarters of the respondents indicated that their job and family life did not *interfere* with each other. In fact, about three-quarters of the respondents indicated that their work and family life had a *positive* effect on each other—either "some" or "a lot"; and that family and friends had provided "some" to "a lot" of support in these elders' efforts to work part-time. Hispanic and white workers reported significantly more family/friend support for their work efforts than did African American workers. As expected, older men maintained that job and family life interfered significantly less often with each other than did older women.

The overall positive relationship between work and family life reported by many respondents may also be related to the fact that almost two-thirds of the elders reported either "rarely" or "never" thinking about their jobs when they were busy doing something else. For one 63-year-old man working in maintenance for a suburban college, the best part about his job was that he didn't take his work home. Although he clearly enjoyed his job at the college, he also valued his free time considerably. Not thinking about their jobs when they were at home was especially the case for older Hispanic workers who, it should be noted, also reported the least amount of interference between their work and family lives.

The views of one agency director served, however, to put the relationship between work and family in some perspective. In her experience, the most common problems that arose were related to health and family responsibilities. This director found that women were more affected by family problems such as having to care for grandchildren whose parents were absent or unable to provide assistance. In similar fashion, another agency director found that the health of the nonworking spouse could also be a major barrier. "We have lost quite a few placements due to older people having to care for a spouse or grandchildren." Most job-placement staff believed that women were more likely to end a placement to care for family members than men, a finding also noted in the literature (Foster and Brizius 1993; Stone, Cafferata, and Sangl 1987).

Another problem unique to Hispanics was either relatively frequent travel to or actually moving back to Puerto Rico. Eighty percent of the elders placed through the Hispanic job-placement program were originally from Puerto Rico, making interruption of work a strong possibility. In her view, most older persons (Hispanics in particular) wished to work in their own neighborhood partly due to safety reasons, but primarily because of language and familiarity. Agency personnel from other sites also cited difficulties with public transportation as problematic for some elder workers.

Working with Others and Job Satisfaction

Respondents were also asked about the satisfaction derived from intergenerational and intragenerational relationships in the workplace. As reported in chapter 8, almost 89 percent of the respondents indicated having the opportunity to work with younger workers on the job. These workers rated their level of overall enjoyment from working with younger workers as 6.1 on a seven-point scale where 1 = none, 3 = a little, 5 = some, and 7 = a lot. Similarly, as reported in chapter 8, the 105 respondents who indicated having opportunities to work with other older part-time workers, reported a mean level of enjoyment of 6.4 on the same seven-point scale. And, of those respondents who did not have opportunities to interact with younger and older workers, about one-third each would have liked more opportunities to associate with younger and same-aged workers on the job.

At least one job-placement program director's views were at odds with these findings. He indicated that a number of elder workers felt they were "not up to the challenge of working with a younger population because they tend to work faster." He pointed out that these older workers were likely to end up quite frustrated because they "feel they are not accomplishing as much as they did in the past." He went on to say that overall, regardless of age or minority status, most of the workers "go with the thought that they will have to work harder because they are old." Some further inconsistencies in this regard are also reported in chapter 10.

Desired Fringe Benefits and Part-Time Work

The fact that most workers received minimal fringe benefits was already reported in chapter 7. While some SCSEP workers did receive sick time, vacation, and paid holidays, some SCSEP workers and most non-SCSEP workers employed in the private sector did not get any benefits. In response to the question of whether there were any fringe benefits they were not getting now that they would like to receive, close to two-thirds responded in the affirmative.

Table 7 presents those fringe benefits that our respondents would have most liked to receive. Medical, surgical, and hospital insurance was the most frequently desired benefit, mentioned by about 55 percent of those responding to this question. Paid vacations and holidays, eye care and dental benefits, and paid sick leave were also desired benefits, mentioned on average about 25 percent of time. Least frequently requested workplace benefits included pensions/annuities, free/discounted meals and merchandise, education and training programs, and profit-sharing opportunities.

However, older workers appeared to be realistic about the fact that receiving fringe benefits was unlikely. One 67-year-old woman, working as a receptionist in an outpatient drug and alcohol clinic didn't "ever plan to stop working." While her work site offered no fringe benefits to part-time workers, she felt this to be a minor drawback. What was important to her was that employers respect the life experience of older employees. She considered this an important intangible benefit in her job.

Satisfaction with Other Facets of Part-Time Work

What difficulties were experienced in terms of travel to and from work and the cost of food at work? In the case of the cost of purchas-

Table 7 Fringe Benefits Lower-Income, Part-Time Employees Would Most Like to Receive*

Fringe Benefits	Frequency Mentioned	
	Number	Percentage
1. Medical, surgical, or hospital insurance	54	54.5
2. Paid vacation	26	26.3
3. Paid holidays	24	24.2
4. Eyeglass or eye care benefits	22	22.2
5. Sick leave with full pay	21	21.1
6. Dental benefits	20	20.2
7. Other	16	16.2
8. Life insurance	10	10.1
9. Pension/Annuity	5	5.1
10. Free or discounted meals	2	2.0
11. Skills training/education programs	1	1.0
12. Profit sharing	1	1.0
13. Free or discounted merchandise	1	1.0

*Each respondent was able to list up to three fringe benefits.

ing food during the workday, difficulties were minimal. Almost nine of every ten workers indicated having no problem at all with the expense associated with eating during the workday. On the other hand, problems associated with traveling to and from work proved more common. Common concerns voiced by the 40 percent who did have a problem included issues of cost, fear of vandalism and crime, and hardship associated with bad weather.

According to one job-placement director, many older workers were dismayed by the "hassles of transportation." For example, a 61-year-old African American woman felt that she could be of more help if she worked more hours as a teacher's assistant in a local child-care facility. However, she admitted that even if the agency budget allowed for extended hours, later hours would make her fearful of travel because she had to commute through a high-crime area on her way to and from work.

However, for some elders, the drawbacks associated with travel could be compensated for, in part, by a satisfying job. One 67-year-old African American woman, working as a kitchen aide in a senior-citizen's center, said her main satisfaction in life came from her work.

Travel usually took about one-and-one-half hours round-trip and involved two bus transfers and much waiting. Even so, this woman was apparently not bothered by the amount of travel time required, rather indicating how much she enjoyed her job for which she was paid $3.70 an hour. Likewise, a 77-year-old white woman, employed as a friendly visitor in the social service department of a senior community center, also didn't mind the fact that she had to take public transportation to all of her clients' homes. She worked 20 hours a week, had a flexible schedule, and very much appreciated not being tied down to an office. She enjoyed having a place to go in the mornings. She also reported that the job fit her personality perfectly in that she "loves cheering up people that are down."

Predictors of Job Satisfaction

In order to determine what variables served as predictors of job satisfaction among these older workers, multiple regression analyses were performed. JSI scores served as the dependent variable in the equation. Based on findings reported in this chapter and in chapters 7 and 8, three categories of independent variables were considered: (1) *demographic variables*, including gender, age, education, household income, and SCSEP and minority status; (2) *personal status variables*, including self-reported happiness and self-reported health concerns; and (3) *work variables*, including hourly wages, satisfaction with days and hours worked per week, fringe-benefit levels, how they perceived younger workers felt about older workers on the job, how they perceived their supervisors felt about older workers, the ability to use existing skills, and the number of other co-workers on the job.

Final regression analysis revealed that 53 percent of the variance in JSI scores could be explained by the following variables, in descending order: the ability to use existing skills; more fringe benefits; the days they worked suiting them; the perception of more positive supervisor attitudes about older workers; their perception of more positive views about older workers by younger workers at their work site; and being of minority status (African American or Hispanic) rather than white.

The Overall Experience of the Job

Several additional questions were included to gauge the overall experience of part-time employment. Asked whether the jobs they had been placed in were what they had expected, the responses were overwhelmingly affirmative. Almost four-fifths of those who responded to this question said that the job was just what they had expected. Close to 20 percent claimed that the job had turned out to be even better than expected.

When asked whether they would decide again to take their part-time job, knowing what they now knew about their job, over four-fifths said they would take their job again without hesitation. When asked what they would miss most about their jobs when they stopped working, over half indicated "being with people." "Remaining busy" was noted 22 percent of the time, and "loss of income," 14 percent of the time. In addition to the importance placed on part-time employment as a source of financial supplementation, opportunities to interact with others and remain active were also clearly important. These findings are also consistent with those in chapter 6, where both unemployed elders and those working part-time strongly endorsed "keeping busy" as an important reason for going to the job-placement agency in the first place.

The multiple benefits of employment were evidenced in the comments of a 67-year-old African American woman who needed the extra money and explained that she was used to low-paying, tedious jobs, with long hours. She tolerated these conditions because "I just don't want to be idle." In the case of a 70-year-old African American woman working as a hospital receptionist, although the salary was an important supplement to her monthly finances, the greatest benefit of her job was its flexibility and the fact that it kept her busy and alert. This woman emphasized how much she liked her job and that "what sounds difficult may not be difficult at all." She was glad she "took the chance." An 84-year-old man, who worked as a senior aide in an inner-city community center, had nothing but positive things to say about his work experience. It was apparent that his part-time job was a very important part of his life. He admitted that once he did stop working (which he hoped wouldn't be for a long time), what he would miss most was the social outlet the job provided. "I love people," he said.

For others, additional income clearly represented the driving force. This was the case for a 73-year-old woman who worked as a clerk, earning $5.25 an hour. In her case, her work was not described as being particularly exciting or satisfying. She worked primarily for financial reasons due to the costs associated with caring for her husband who suffered from dementia and required a great deal of care. However, for another worker, a 65-year-old man who supervised mentally challenged workers at a large oil company, the additional income from his part-time job was a mixed blessing. He pointed out that he is now "financially independent" and buying "too much booze," which angered his wife.

Advice for Others Seeking Part-Time Work

These elders had encouraging advice to give to other older workers contemplating part-time employment. The vast majority of part-time workers urged other elders looking for part-time work to do it regardless of how long they might have been unemployed. The advice of one 75-year-old white male to other older potential workers was: "Do it, it is a good thing," and "Keep looking if you don't find the right job at first." "Get sprucy, feel good about yourself," was the advice of a part-timer employed as a custodian with the Board of Education. Another 63-year-old woman advised the elderly to "try and find a job you'll find satisfying."

Their recommendations for employers were to recognize that older adults were responsible, hard-working, and valued employees rather than charity cases. This rationale has been repeatedly echoed by both employees and employers in public-opinion surveys dealing with older workers (Louis Harris and Associates 1992; American Association of Retired Persons 1989; Yankelovich, Skelly, and White 1985; Gollub 1983).

The advice of one 70-year-old woman for employers was to "look to them [older workers] as human beings, as someone who is capable: instruct them right and they will do the best they can." A 65-year-old woman, working as a licensed practical nurse for a nursing temporary agency, gave this advice for employers considering older workers: "They [older workers] are very smart people." She further maintained that "we seniors are dependable, and do what needs to get done." Another part-timer was convinced that "employers only need to give older workers a chance."

Finally, as mentioned previously in chapter 9, one job-placement agency director spoke of prospective employers needing to learn how to communicate more effectively with older workers and to learn how to convey criticism in a constructive manner. He believed that employers sometimes had difficulty "understanding the issues of the older worker." In his view, employers generally did not have a good understanding of the physical and psychological aspects of aging that could potentially create challenges for both the employee and employer.

Summary

All subgroups of survey respondents as well as job-placement program staff reported relatively high levels of overall job satisfaction for these elder part-time workers. The quality of the physical work environment and the quality of supervision were also strongly endorsed. Hispanics and African Americans did register significantly higher levels of job satisfaction than whites. Difficulties associated with transportation, combined with inadequacies in fringe-benefit packages (in particular, the absence of medical, surgical, and health insurance) appeared to be of greatest concern to workers. Regression analyses indicated that 53 percent of the variance in job satisfaction was accounted for by the following: the receipt of fringe benefits, being able to use existing skills, favorable attitudes toward elder workers by their supervisors and younger workers, and being of minority status.

Respondents reported that time rarely dragged for them on the job and that they put considerable effort into carrying out their work responsibilities. On the other hand, concerns related to the job did not seem to extend beyond the workplace. While a worker's family life did not appear, as a rule, to *interfere* with the job, it was not unusual for family responsibilities (e.g., caring for an infirm spouse or grandchildren) to surface periodically and demand the attention of these employees, especially the women.

Enjoyment levels associated with interaction with younger workers as well as same-aged peers on the job were relatively high. Furthermore, a good proportion of those who did not have opportunities to interact with others at work wished they did. Even so, according to job-placement program staff, complaints about relationships at work were not unusual.

Based on their experience, if given the opportunity to do it over again, a clear majority of workers would again accept their current part-time jobs. Employment for these individuals served the dual function of providing needed additional income and enabling these individuals to remain active and socially engaged. These workers endorsed the idea of part-time employment, felt older people made an important contribution while on the job, and encouraged other elders and prospective employers to embrace part-time work for older citizens.

Given overall job satisfaction, another check should clearly be placed under the "good" part-time job column.

Chapter Ten
Discrimination in the Workplace

Soumerai and Avorn (1983) and others (Golden 1992; National Commission on Working Women 1987; Morrison 1986; Kahne 1985) have argued that older persons are exceedingly vulnerable to inadequate salaries and other forms of exploitation. The deleterious effects of age and gender discrimination, in particular, have been well documented (see, for example, Kuriansky and Porter forthcoming; Christensen 1990; Porter 1995; Rosen and Jerdee 1995; Weiss 1989; Herz and Rones 1989; Meier 1988; Shaw 1988; 9 to 5 1987, 1986). When elder workers engage in part-time employment they become, according to others (Olmsted 1985), subject to additional discrimination.

The fact that many employees have ambivalent attitudes about older workers (Peterson and Wendt 1995; Barth, McNaught, and Rizzi 1995, 1993) and that elders are routinely excluded from training programs (Barth, McNaught, and Rizzi 1995, 1993) has also been well documented. Although legal remedies to redress age and gender discrimination are in place (Porter and Kuriansky forthcoming; Bessey and Srijati 1991), there is also evidence that legal cases are not being brought forward by low-income elder workers. For example, even though the number of age-discrimination cases brought before the Equal Employment Opportunity Commission increased by close to 30 percent between 1989 and 1993, most of the complainants were male professionals. According to Bass, Quinn, and Burkhauser (1995): ". . . it is questionable whether the courts offer a viable means of ensuring employment at older age for either men or women who are less sophisticated in the legal process" (p. 284).

Similar patterns have been noted around gender-discrimination suits for older female workers. In many of these cases, plaintiffs have also been women in upper-level management and professional positions, with the majority of cases routinely settled before trial (Kuriansky and Porter forthcoming; Weiss 1989). For the low-income older male or female worker experiencing age and/or gender discrimination, the conclusion that legal remedies are largely a "practical impossibility" (Kuriansky and Porter forthcoming) seems well taken.

To what extent did elder workers in our study report discrimination on the basis of age, gender, race, or national origin in their relationships at work? Did they perceive themselves to be discriminated against because they worked part-time? Did agency placement personnel perceive any of the above forms of discrimination against older workers? These questions are addressed in this chapter.

In order to gauge levels of discrimination in lower-income employment, older workers were asked a series of questions to assess the extent of perceived age discrimination, part-time work discrimination, and workplace bias based on gender, race, and national origin. Data about discrimination were also gathered through interviews with job-placement staff and older workers. The limited number of respondents reporting any degree of discrimination of any kind on our indices precluded meaningful analyses of differences in the experience of discrimination by age, gender, race, and SCSEP status.

At the same time, there was an obvious disjuncture between the responses to the indices, which revealed minimal perceived discrimination of any sort, and some of the qualitative impressions of agency informants and anecdotal remarks of the elder workers themselves. These discrepancies are also addressed.

Age Discrimination in Lower-Income Employment

Only 7 percent, or 11 respondents, indicated that they felt in any way discriminated against on the job because of their age. And of these 11, only three said it was a "sizable problem." An additional six persons felt it represented a "slight problem" in their work.

In order to determine the specific ways in which older workers might feel discriminated against because of their age, the 11 persons who reported some degree of age bias were asked to respond to a series of seven statements gauging the ways in which such discrimination was expressed. These seven statements comprised the Age

Discrimination Index in which responses were scored from 1 to 4, where 1 = a statement that was "not at all true" to 4 = a statement that was believed to be "very true." The items in the index were:

1. I feel I'm not given respect.
2. I feel that I will receive fewer promotions than younger workers.
3. I feel that I've been given a "bad" job (e.g., undesirable work assignment).
4. I felt discriminated against in "hiring" practices. (It's hard to get hired if you're my age.)
5. I feel discriminated against in performance evaluations. (My work is watched more closely than that of younger workers.)
6. I feel there are salary inequities between workers my age and younger workers. (Younger workers get paid more.)
7. I feel I receive fewer fringe benefits than younger workers.

Scores for all of the individual items, except for item #2, as well as the composite index score, fell below the midpoint, confirming that age discrimination was not reported to play a major role in the employment experience, even for the 7 percent of workers who reported some degree of age discrimination on the job. The only item scored above the midpoint (x=2.4) was #2: "I feel that I will receive fewer promotions than younger workers.

Discrimination Due to Gender, Race, and National Origin
Respondents also assessed the extent of perceived bias at work on the basis of gender, race, and national origin. The occurrence of such discrimination was even less commonly reported than ageism. No respondents reported being in any way discriminated against on the job because of their sex. Five persons (3 percent) felt discriminated against for racial reasons and the same number felt that national origin was the basis of workplace bias. However, only three of the five reported that racial discrimination was even a "slight problem" for them and only one person felt bias due to national origin constituted a "great problem." Two of the five workers who had experienced racial discrimination and four of the five workers who

had experienced national origin discrimination maintained that the experience was "no problem at all" for them.

Part-Time Work Discrimination

To assess perceived discrimination on the basis of working part-time, all respondents were asked to complete an 11-item Part-Time Work Discrimination Index. Scored on a four-point scale, where a higher score reflected greater perceived bias, the Part-Time Work Discrimination Index had excellent reliability (alpha = 0.88).

Table 8 presents the mean scores for all respondents on the individual items of the index, as well as on the composite score. Similar to perceived discrimination based on age, gender, race, and national origin, part-time work discrimination was extremely limited. Individual index item mean scores as well as the composite index score fell well below the statistical midpoint, with all statements rated as "not at all true" or "not very true." As in the case of reported age discrimination, the belief that part-time work status would serve to reduce opportunities for promotions was the highest-ranking statement. As true in the Age Discrimination Index, this item was also scored in the lower quadrant of the possible score range.

Levels of perceived part-time work discrimination did not differ significantly across the various categories of part-time employees. It was similarly low for all older workers regardless of gender, race/ethnicity, age, and SCSEP status. When asked to assess the extent to which part-time work discrimination was a problem for respondents, 95.5 percent said it was "no problem at all." Seven respondents (4.5 percent) assessed it as being "a slight problem." No one reported it to be a "sizable" or "great" problem.

Table 8 Ways in Which Part-Time Work Discrimination Is Felt (Part-Time Work Discrimination Index)

Ways Part-Time Work Discrimination Is Felt	Mean*
1. I feel I'm not given respect.	1.2
2. I feel that I will receive fewer promotions than others.	1.6
3. I feel that I've been given a "bad" job—(undesirable work assignment).	1.1
4. I felt discriminated against in "hiring" practices. (It's hard to get hired if you're my age.)	1.2
5. I feel discriminated against in performance evaluations.	

Ways Part-Time Work Discrimination Is Felt	Mean[a]
(My work is watched more closely than that of younger workers.)	1.1
6. I sometimes feel like a second-class citizen because I work part-time.	1.2
7. Older full-time workers think I'm not as capable because I work part-time.	1.1
8. Younger full-time workers think I'm not as capable because I work part-time.	1.2
9. Older full-time workers feel I don't work as hard because I work part-time.	1.1
10. Younger full-time workers feel I don't work as hard because I work part-time.	1.2
11. I feel isolated because I work part-time.	1.1
Index Score[a]	1.2
SD = 0.43, alpha = 0.88	

[a]Individual item and index score range 1–4, where 1 = not at all true, 2 = not very true, 3 = somewhat true, and 4 = very true.

Qualitative Data on Workplace Discrimination: Views from Agency Personnel

While some of the literature cited in the beginning of this chapter indicated that discrimination based on age, gender, and national origin was commonplace in the workplace, how do we account for the fact that our respondents reported almost no discrimination of any kind on our indices? Perhaps as Rayman, Allshouse, and Allen (1993) have pointed out:

Discrimination, whether based on age, sex, or race is one of the most difficult labor market influences to identify and quantify. Age discrimination is particularly elusive, because it is often subtle and subconscious: employers discriminating against older people may not be aware they are doing so, and those being discriminated against can be incognizant of the situation. (p. 143)

Data drawn from in-person interviews with job-placement agency directors and staff as well as some anecdotal evidence from older workers challenged our blanket finding of little or no bias of any kind on our discrimination indices. At the same time, there was also some support for the fact that discrimination was often subtle, and sometimes not done consciously. Drawing upon these qualitative data, the overall consensus from agency personnel and the majority of elder workers was that discrimination, while more prevalent than our indices revealed, was still not a major issue for the majority of elder workers. Some examples follow.

Job-placement agency staff generally agreed that employers hired the most qualified person for the job and that age, in most cases, was not a major factor. At the same time, however, they recognized that some employers were looking for "young-old" workers between the ages of 50 and 60. One staff person recalled that an employer who contacted the agency about a position said: "I know I'm not supposed to say this but please send us someone young." According to another agency key informant, most of the elders were well aware of this sentiment and "go with the thought that they will have to work harder because they are *old*."

Another agency director felt there was some discrimination in terms of promotions in both the private sector and in the nonprofit agencies. In the subsidized jobs, "they are not thought of as potential employees and are not given legitimate training opportunities. Sometimes they support you and sometimes they let you drift." In the private sector, this director felt that discrimination occurred most frequently in hiring practices rather than after the person was employed. He went on to say that "none of this is overt, of course" but the job-placement agency learned of such occurrences because the older employees would frequently bring it to their attention. In fact, in some cases, older workers were very open about discussing discrimination with agency staff and appeared quite sensitive to instances of discrimination.

In the SCSEP jobs, a coordinator was responsible for making periodic visits to the employee's work site to evaluate the placement. This provided the employee and employer an opportunity to provide feedback. In the private sector, however, it was typically left to the employee to contact the job placement program if discrimination occurred on the job.

When an employment program learned of an alleged case of discrimination, they did not automatically stop using that particular employer for other placements. Rather, potential new workers were likely to be informed of the prior worker's experience at that particular job site. At the same time, because of the scarcity of potential job sites, there was pressure to continue to use employers, even in the face of alleged instances of discrimination.

No formal evaluation processes had been established in these job-placement programs to deal with cases of discrimination. Cases were likely to surface only when employees took the initiative and voiced their concern.

The key informant from the agency serving the Hispanic elderly reported that Hispanic community agencies generally had a strong interest in helping older Hispanic workers. As a result, she felt discrimination was not as apparent in these settings as in other agencies because Hispanics had "a lot of respect for the older person in our culture." She went on to say that Hispanic community agencies wanted to protect the older workers to the extent that employers would not give older employees certain tasks to perform, fearing that they might hurt themselves. An example cited was not allowing an older worker to climb a ladder to change a light bulb.

In this instance, there appeared a sincere desire to protect the older worker, yet at the same time, this action could also be interpreted as patronizing. In this staffer's experience, discrimination was more readily apparent in non-Hispanic agencies. One potential employer was cited who "will not even consider hiring an Hispanic employee though they go through the application process and play the game." According to another agency respondent: "Hispanics are discriminated against anyway; add to that age, and add to that language barriers. . . ."

In some other cases, employers had sensed the older person's need to secure a job to be so great that they would sometimes give the older person a job that no one else wanted to do. An example was a public agency which hired an older worker as a messenger but reassigned him to clean toilets because nobody else would do the job.

There was another form of discrimination related to part-time employment status mentioned by one agency director. He observed that older part-time workers were sometimes excluded from social activities at work such as Christmas parties because they were not viewed as regular employees. This was believed to be more likely in some of the subsidized placements because the workers were not paid directly by the employer. We did not inquire whether such action was common across work sites.

Finally, a job-placement agency director recalled one white woman who repeatedly felt discriminated against by various employers and was never satisfied. It was eventually discovered that this woman did not like working with African Americans and that this was the source of the problem, rather than her experiencing discrimination herself.

Views from Elder Workers

While agency directors and staff tended to minimize the extent of discrimination against older African American workers by employers, a few older persons who were interviewed presented a contrary view, one which has been documented in the literature (Kuriansky and Porter forthcoming; Rayman, Allshouse, and Allen 1993). One 65-year-old African American divorcee who described herself as an accomplished musician and music-school entrepreneur, indicated that she has found it extremely difficult to find work. She wanted to work but felt discriminated against because of her race. Even so, she admitted that this was "not a huge problem."

Another 59-year-old African American woman who was widowed and had been working for more than a year as a data-entry clerk for a community newspaper found the job very pleasing but had some concerns about not being respected, salary inequities, and racial discrimination. In spite of these concerns, however, she liked her work and had apparently found other ways to compensate for what she felt was lacking on the job.

Still another 73-year-old white female reported that when she began her job search, she would inquire if the employers were only looking for young people because she did not want to waste her own time and effort. She further remarked that she felt as though people "tend to look at us like we're slower." When this woman accepted her present clerical job, she continued to feel somewhat discriminated against and feared being passed over for job promotions because of her age "until they got to know me better."

There were several examples of two-way and reverse discrimination where older persons claimed to experience bias, yet also showed evidence of bias in their own behaviors and beliefs. For example, one 66-year-old white male had recently retired from his cook's-helper job at a fast-food restaurant. He expressed considerable bitterness about this type of work, feeling he got no respect and was discriminated against because of his age. He believed that the high-school kids he worked with were lazy and "mostly drug addicts." He was angry about the lack of periodic raises and evaluations and the fact that there were no paid vacations or holidays. He claimed "the management at these places don't know what they are doing—they don't listen to their employees and they hire undependable, lazy help." He made a plea that older people are "more stable, patriotic, courteous, and prompt—hire them!"

Summary

In response to our discrimination indices, almost all of the older persons surveyed indicated that they had not experienced discrimination of any type during the course of their application for and engagement in part-time employment. Discrimination due to age and part-time work status was perceived to be only slightly more common than discrimination based on the older worker's gender, race, or national origin. Discrimination, when present, was expressed in terms of reduced salaries and fewer promotions for older workers. Even for those persons who said they had experienced discriminatory behavior in the workplace, such occurrences were not reported as a significant problem for them.

At the same time, however, there were more indirect indications in the passing remarks of some elders and key informants that age discrimination clearly existed in the workplace. We should be mindful of Herz and Rones' conclusion (1989) in this regard that "age discrimination exists regarding older workers' employment and advancement opportunities. Nevertheless, relatively few older workers state that they have been victims of age discrimination. . . ." (p. 20)

Agency directors and staff tended to agree that discrimination in the workplace did not constitute a major stumbling block for older persons seeking employment. Even so, many examples were cited of discriminatory behavior by employers based on age, part-time work status, and race/ethnicity, in that order. Job-placement programs seemed to have less control over discriminatory practices in the private sector, yet examples of discrimination also occurred in SCSEP programs as well.

Such discriminatory actions could be subtle, as the literature has also documented. Because employers were valuable commodities, they were not easily removed from agency placement lists, even when discrimination complaints were voiced. Hispanic community agencies were reported to demonstrate greater allegiance to the hiring of older Hispanics, though in some cases, this loyalty bordered on overly protective behavior toward the older worker. Formal evaluation procedures for addressing cases of discrimination had not been established by any of the job-placement programs studied.

At the same time, both agency personnel and elder workers indicated that the existence of the job-placement program did provide a buffer against age discrimination, at least in initial hiring. As one agency informant put it: "We spare the older person from going through hoops to find jobs." "They don't want to go on a job search and that is why they come to us." Similarly a grateful elder worker responded that by going through a job agency, "the employer knows what he's getting before you go. You don't have to explain how old you are. That's already been done." Or as another 69-year-old white male put it: "I went off on my own a couple of times—you can feel the undercurrent. They expected someone younger and they give you elaborate explanations of why they can't hire you. . . . But the placement agency makes no bones about it—they are a good bridge." Or as another 76-year-old white male put it: "The agency is very helpful. Otherwise you'd have to go to a particular office to see if they had a job."

Finally, it may also be as Henretta (1994) has suggested, that the generally low level of reported discrimination was due to the fact that:

Employers are less likely to discriminate against older workers in part-time or temporary work because such jobs are not entry portals to careers carrying fringe benefits, training, and implicit commitment. (p. 75)

Chapter Eleven
Work and Retirement
Attitudes, Preferences, and Expectations

Data presented in this chapter address the attitudes of older part-time employees toward work and retirement. The following issues are addressed: (1) preferences for working part-time versus full-time; (2) the relative value assigned to work; (3) job-placement directors' views about the work expectations of elders; (4) those factors contributing to the retirement decision; and (5) elders' views about the ability to manage in the absence of salaried employment.

The Decision to Work Part-Time Rather Than Full-Time
Several questions were posed to elders about their decision to work in part-time rather than full-time jobs. What reasons did they give? Slightly more than one in every five persons (23 percent) indicated that they wanted more time to do the things they enjoyed. Part-time work allowed them this opportunity. Slightly fewer had chosen part-time work because of Social Security restrictions on allowable income (16 percent); limitations imposed by their own poor health (11 percent); the fact that they didn't want the "hassles" of full-time work (11 percent); and the belief that full-time jobs were not available to them (13 percent). Less commonly cited reasons included the responsibilities imposed by the poor health of a spouse, the demands of other personal and family problems, and the fact that the job-placement programs were geared toward part-time positions.

In addition, in response to the question about whether they would prefer to work full-time, about three-quarters of the respondents said no. Just as presented in chapter 6, all of these results confirmed that part-time work was chosen *voluntarily* for about three-quarters of our respondents—e.g., not because full-time work was not available or because of slack economic conditions. At the same time, there were some exceptions. For example, for a 75-year-old white male working as an advocate for elderly victims at a local organization for the aging, part-time work was not his first choice. While he felt "somewhat valuable" in his present position, he would also have preferred to work full-time, since for him, "work is the most meaningful part of life."

Attitudes toward Work

In order to gauge the relative value placed on work, respondents were given a series of attitudinal statements. These 14 items comprised the Attitude Toward Work Index (ATWI), previously developed by Goodwin (1972). Scored on a four-point scale in which 1 = strongly disagree, 2 = disagree, 3 = agree, and 4 = strongly agree, this index had good internal reliability (alpha = 0.88)

As presented in Table 9, respondents reported consistently positive attitudes toward work. The overall index score was in the upper quartile, representing responses that were clustered both near to or above the "agree" ranking on the scoring scale. Respondents agreed most strongly with the following statements: (1) "I feel good when I have a job"; (2) "Work is a good builder of character"; and (3) "To me, it is important in a job that a person be able to see the results of their own work." While there were no significant differences by age or gender, both Hispanic workers and SCSEP enrollees reported a significantly stronger commitment to work than African Americans or whites, and workers who were not SCSEP enrollees.

These results are consistent with those of other survey efforts around the time of our data collection (see, for example, 9 to 5 1987; American Association of Retired Persons 1986). These national surveys revealed continued high levels of commitment of older workers to the work ethic. AARP's 1989 survey of businesses' response to older workers also reported an increased appreciation of this fact by employers. To quote: "Older workers view themselves as possessing superior work habits and commitment, and believe that management recognizes their strong work ethic" (American Association of Retired Persons 1989, p. 6).

As part of the Commonwealth Fund's The Americans Over 55 at Work Program, attitudinal surveys conducted by Louis Harris and Associates in 1991 and 1992 continued to reveal elders' strong

Table 9 Attitudes of Part-Time Employees toward Work (Attitudes toward Work Index)

Attitudes toward Work Items	Mean*
1. Most people like to work.	3.3
2. I'd be happiest if I didn't have to work at all.	3.2
3. If I don't have a regular job, I don't feel right.	3.1
4. I feel good when I have a job.	3.6
5. Getting recognition for my job is important to me.	3.4
6. My main satisfaction in life comes from my work.	2.9
7. People can't really think well of themselves unless they have a job.	2.8
8. To me, it's important to have the kind of job that gives me a chance to develop my own special abilities.	3.4
9. Work is a good builder of character.	3.6
10. To me, gaining the respect of family and friends is one of the important rewards of getting ahead in a job.	3.2
11. Hard work makes you a better person.	3.2
12. Success in a job is mainly a matter of hard work.	3.1
13. To me, it's important in a job that a person be able to see the results of their own work.	3.6
14. Success in a job is mainly a matter of how much you know.	3.0
Total Index Score	3.2

SD = 0.51, alpha = 0.88

*Individual item and index score range 1–4, where a higher score indicates greater agreement with the statement(s).

commitment to work, stronger, in fact, than is commonly recognized (McNaught 1994). These Louis Harris surveys also reported a continuing desire on the part of elders for the expansion of part-time work options (Commonwealth Fund 1993).

At the same time, results from *Labor Force 2000* (Barth, McNaught, and Rizzi 1993), a survey of 406 human-resource executives from major corporations, and also part of The Americans Over 55 at Work Program, are both instructive and troubling. Even though seniors were consistently rated by these resource managers as reliable, loyal, and having consistently positive attitudes toward work, managers' attitudes about the overall performance of older workers was described as "ambivalent" (Barth, McNaught, and Rizzi 1993, p. 162). Based on the same and additional management surveys, McNaught (1994) reported that "employers were seen as stereotyping them [older workers] as loyal and possessing good work habits, but inflexible and difficult to train" (p. 229). As discussed in chapter 10, ageism remains an often subtle, yet seemingly intractable phenomenon in the workplace.

Work Expectations of Elders: The Views of Job-Placement Directors

According to job-placement directors, older adults generally had valid expectations about certain aspects of working and less accurate perceptions of others. The key informant from the agency serving primarily Hispanic elderly reported that applicants generally had realistic expectations of the function of the placement program. To encourage a realistic view of obtainable jobs, participants were informed by staff early on about what to expect in terms of salary, jobs, and benefits. This indoctrination process was very helpful, according to another job-placement program director, in helping elders become aware of what to expect in the workplace.

If there was an area of distorted thinking on the part of some elders, it was around salary expectations. For those paid with Title V funds, the same hourly wage was paid regardless of the type of work performed. As a result, some participants felt that it was unfair that the more skilled jobs, such as some entry-level administrative positions, were compensated at the same rate as the more unskilled jobs, such as janitorial work.

The director of the program serving older Hispanics also felt that community agencies that served primarily Hispanics had more realistic expectations about older workers. However, she also reported that this realistic appraisal was primarily the case because these agencies were not paying for the elders' services and therefore had lower expectations. On the other hand, agencies with unsubsidized jobs had higher expectations for workers because they had a direct financial stake in them.

According to another job-placement official, some employers were not realistic about what to expect from older workers. They sometimes expected a higher skill level, educational background, and energy level than they received. This director concurred that employer expectations also varied according to whether the placement was subsidized or not. With subsidized positions, expectations were lower, since they had a "free person and will accept whatever they produce."

Retirement Issues

Table 10 presents the views of part-timers on an additional set of items, gauging attitudes toward work and retirement, taken from the 1971 wave of the Social Security Retirement History Study (Irelan, Rabin, and Schwab 1987). Once again study respondents demonstrated a strong commitment to the work ethic in their responses to this scale. They agreed most with items referring to the various benefits assigned to working status (items 4–7, where means ranged from 3.0 to 3.4). While the advantages of retirement (as illustrated in items 1–3) were acknowledged, mean scores on these items (ranging from 2.4 to 2.9) reflected a cautious response about the attractiveness of this stage of life. Respondents were least likely to agree that "older workers should retire when they can, so as to give younger people more of a chance on the job."

Hence, even though retirement is often depicted as harmonious, meeting the needs of employers and employees alike, our re-

Table 10 Attitudes about Work and Retirement by Part-Time Employees

Attitudinal Statement	Mean*
1. Retirement is a pleasant time of life.	2.9
2. People who don't retire when they can afford to are foolish.	2.6
3. Older workers should retire when they can, so as to give younger people more of a chance on the job.	2.4
4. Work is the most meaningful part of life.	3.0
5. Most people think more of someone who works than they do of someone who doesn't.	3.1
6. A good, secure income is more important than the chance of getting raises.	3.2
7. A chance for promotion is an important part of any good job.	3.4

*Mean item score range 1–4, where a higher score reflects greater agreement with the statement (1 = strongly disagree, 2 = disagree, 3 = agree, and 4 = strongly agree).

spondents' views were at odds with this rather facile conclusion. Although the decision to retire used to be viewed more as a consequence of the declining health or physical capabilities of older people or because of mandatory retirement rules, retirement is now viewed as a more complex process involving assessment of: (1) the psychological and monetary rewards of continued work versus the value of leisure time; (2) the need to finance the remainder of life; and (3) the desire to withdraw from the labor force gradually (Barth, McNaught, and Rizzi 1995).

For working-class and low-income elders, there is clear evidence that economic survival is a dominant force. In one of the few studies of working-class retirees, Calasanti and Bonanno (1992) cited extensive evidence showing that the strongest predictor of work among union and nonunion, as well as male and female retirees, was low income. They further concluded that "the greatest discrepancy between the ideal and reality of retirement appears among the working class" (p. 135).

Additional alarm has been raised recently about inadequate retirement income for minorities and women, such as those in our study. For example, recent statistics from the National Caucus and Center on Black Aged, Inc. (1994), revealed that aggregate retirement income for African Americans was significantly less than for whites. Elderly African Americans were nearly four times as likely than elderly white men to have annual incomes less than $5,000. Aged African American females were almost twice as likely to have annual incomes less than $5,000 than white women. There is a similarly grim picture for older Hispanics. According to 1991 Census Bureau figures, 10.3 percent of whites, compared with 33.8 percent of African Americans and 20.8 percent of Hispanics, were living in poverty (Garcia 1993).

The retirement situation for older women, in particular, is alarming. According to the Older Women's League's 1995 Mother's Day Report (Porter 1995), only 13 percent of women 65 and over received pensions. Their incomes were further reduced by the penalty in Social Security for years out of the work force. Older African American and Hispanic women were especially vulnerable to poverty after age 65. The authors concluded that precisely the factors that made it difficult for female workers to qualify for private pensions—limited hours, low wages, and moving in and out of the labor force in primarily nonunion service jobs—were precisely the same factors that caused women to receive lower Social Security retirement benefits. Equally alarming is the fact that three in five younger women today hold jobs in sales, clerical, and service positions, making it likely that many of today's younger women will have no more economic security in old age than their grandmothers and mothers had.

As Kahn (1994) has pointed out, however, this discrepancy between the ideal and the reality of retirement is a more generalized phenomenon, extending well beyond the working class and those living in poverty:

> . . . the allegation of universal prosperity among older people is greatly exaggerated. . . . The dollar income of elderly households (occupants 60 year of age or more) is less than two-thirds (64 percent) that of younger households. If adjusted for household size, however, money income is about equal for these two age groups. With a further adjustment for nonmoney income and assets, the advantage shifts to older people because of Medicare, pension entitlements, and equity in housing. The situation of older people varies greatly, however. Only 15 percent have financial assets in addition to those just listed, and more than 12 percent have incomes below the poverty line. (pp. 43–44)

The extent of retirement anxiety was also expressed recently by respondents, aged 51–60, who are part of the National Institute on Aging's recently launched longitudinal study, addressing retirement issues of the baby-boom generation. About 40 percent of this group reported that they would have no income other than Social Security when they retired. Further, over half felt that in the event of a layoff, they could lose their present job within a year, with almost half reporting less than a 50–50 chance of finding a new job (National Institute on Aging 1993). Similar worry and anxiety were also reported recently by middle to upper-middle income individuals in a *New York Times* article (Uchitelle 1995), entitled "Retirement's Worried Face." Regardless of social class standing, many Americans clearly do not anticipate retirement as a relaxed or pleasant time of life, but rather one likely to include significant financial anxiety, such as our respondents expressed.

The Decision to Retire

Elders were also queried about their retirement expectations. Posed with a scenario in which they inherited enough money to live comfortably without working, two out of three of those responding to this hypothetical situation (95, or 65 percent) claimed they would still choose to work. Furthermore, of those respondents who indicated that a compulsory retirement age existed in their current jobs, well over two-thirds insisted they would continue to work if their employers let them. Only one in ten workers who faced compulsory retirement rules in their jobs (11.5 percent) indicated that they planned to retire before that age was reached.

Of course, not all respondents were aware of their employer's retirement policy. This was the case for a 63-year-old widow working as a clerk in the personnel office of a large corporation. She was unaware of a fixed retirement-age policy in her company and was looking forward to working as long as she was able. For her, the reward of employment was "the opportunity to interact with others, keep my mind active, and feel useful."

It is noteworthy that 67.5 percent of all elders surveyed indicated that they did not expect to stop working at a regular job. These individuals clearly indicated that they would seek other employment if they were pressed to leave their current positions. In fact, the vast majority of respondents (91 percent) claimed that they would continue to seek part-time employment when they stop working at a regular job.

Of those who mentioned a specific age when they expected to stop working at a regular job, the majority specified ages which were in the 70- to 80-year range, with a median of 77 years. These are ages when the vast majority of workers have vacated the labor market (Parnes and Summers 1994). However, Parnes and Summers' study of the work experiences of men in their seventies and eighties, who had shunned retirement, found that "good health, a strong psychological commitment to work, and a corresponding distaste for retirement are among the most important characteristics related to continued employment into old age" (p. 5117). These were all qualities characterizing the majority of those in our study who were working part-time.

For those part-timers who reported the intention to stop working in a regular job at a particular age, the most common reason (mentioned more than twice as often as any other) was personal health. The desire to retire in order to enjoy leisure activities was mentioned less frequently. Being too old or too tired to work or the ability to collect a pension or Social Security benefits were rarely cited as reasons to retire at a particular age. The attitude of one 64-year-old woman was not uncommon. She worked in a clerical job for a nonprofit organization which informed citizens about various political issues and encouraged voter registration. She planned to keep working until "at least the age of 80," but might even work a little after retirement if she needed the income and her health permitted. In similar fashion, a 63-year-old woman working a 30-hour-a-week job as an activities aide in a nursing home was in no hurry to stop working and planned to continue as long as possible.

Like others described above, the ability to manage financially in retirement for these workers was colored by considerable anxiety. Close to half anticipated having financial problems during the course of their retirement years. Almost six out of every ten elders expected their expenses to be the same as they were now. Smaller but equal proportions were anticipating their expenses to be either more or less than now (20 percent and 21 percent, respectively).

Asked how they would manage financially during the course of retirement, fully one-third of these part-timers indicated they would work a little and/or collect government benefits. About 17 percent anticipated needing help from relatives. Given their very modest household incomes, these concerns seem well warranted. If Siegel (1993) is correct that "most workers choose to retire when they think they can afford it" (p. 452), it seems quite reasonable to anticipate that many of our respondents will have to "work till they die."

Summary

A variety of factors were operative in respondents' decisions to work part-time, including the wish for more time to do enjoyable things; Social Security restrictions; the sense that full-time jobs were likely to be more stressful or else not available; and poor health. Although all categories of older workers reported a relatively strong commitment toward work, this was especially characteristic of minorities (Hispanics in particular) and SCSEP workers.

The work ethic appeared well ingrained in our respondents; few elders were considering retirement any time soon. In fact, if employers allowed them, most would continue working past an organization's compulsory retirement age. The anticipated age of retirement for those contemplating it was in the 70- to 80-year range, a time when the vast majority of American workers have already stopped working. Reasons for stopping work at a particular age were most frequently related to concerns about poor health and to a lesser degree, the wish to enjoy leisure activities.

As is true of many Americans today, across the economic spectrum, our respondents reported considerable concern about how they would manage financially in retirement. More likely than not, expenses were expected to stay the same or increase during that stage of life rather than decline, with a likely scenario that most of these individuals would never be in a position to withdraw from the labor force with any level of financial comfort. Many would need to "work till they die."

Chapter Twelve
The Special Case of the Unemployed

We begin by reviewing pertinent findings from chapters 4, 5, and 6 about the background characteristics, prior work experience, and experience with the job-placement agency for the 80 unemployed interviewees. The next section describes the immediate circumstances surrounding the last job before unemployment, including an examination of any differences by age, gender, minority, and SCSEP status. The third section begins with vignettes describing the particular circumstances of job departure for some of the unemployed elders. The chapter closes with some reflections from key agency personnel about why close to a third of those workers placed in part-time positions in fiscal 1987 were unemployed by the time they were interviewed—at most two years later.

Review of Background Characteristics, Prior Work Experience, and Job Placement Experience

On average, the unemployed were likely to be female, over age 65, of minority backgrounds (42 percent African American, 14 percent Hispanic), and with a high-school education or more. The majority had household incomes less than $9,000; about one-quarter had household incomes less than $5,000. About one-third were married, one-third widowed, and the rest separated, divorced, or single. About 40 percent lived alone. There were no significant differences between the unemployed and part-timers on any of these characteristics. However, there were significant differences in terms of perceived health status and life satisfaction. On the whole, the unemployed saw themselves as more limited in the kind of work they could do, reported somewhat less energy overall, and worried more about their physical health. Likewise, as a group, the unemployed reported less satisfaction with the way they were living and less happiness overall.

On the whole, the unemployed had considerable work histories, which were not different in the aggregate from those of the part-timers. Their longest job had been full-time, in clerical and/or sales, or service positions, where they had worked for around 16 years. They had left this position for a variety of reasons, including the job ending, their poor health, and in fewer instances, because of retirement. They had been out of work four to five years on average before coming to the placement agency.

Like the part-timers, the majority of unemployed elders were looking for clerical, sales, and service positions from the placement agencies, which they by and large received. Like the part-timers, the most important reasons for their application to the placement agency were to keep busy, to work part-time, and to supplement their income. Significantly more of the unemployed than part-timers left the agency placement job for health reasons or because they wanted to work less. Likewise, significantly more of the unemployed elders reported not receiving the job they wanted from the placement agency.

The Last Job before Unemployment

As a group, the unemployed had been out of work, on average, ten months, regardless of age, minority, or SCSEP status. For almost 80 percent of the unemployed, their last job had been the placement agency job, regardless of gender, age, or minority status. For former SCSEP workers, however, the percentage was significantly greater— for over 90 percent, their last job had been the agency job. For almost 80 percent of the unemployed, this last job had been in clerical, sales, or service work, regardless of age or SCSEP status. Like the part-timers, significantly more women than men and more whites than African Americans and Hispanics had been in clerical and sales positions, while more Hispanics and African Americans than whites had been in service positions. On average, the unemployed had worked between 20 and 25 hours a week in this last job, which they held about a year, again with no differences by age, gender, or minority or SCSEP status. The mean hourly pay at the time they left this job was $4.93.

There were a variety of reasons reported for leaving this last job, with no one of them accounting for a large percentage of elders, nor with any significant variations by age, gender, or minority or SCSEP status. About one-quarter left either because of their poor health or that of a relative, or involuntarily—because they were laid off, the job was seasonal, or the employer went out of business. Only about 5 percent left because of retirement. Around 11 percent left because they wanted to work less. The majority of the unemployed reported leaving this job at their own initiative and were not currently looking for another job.

For those who were looking for another job, the majority were looking for a part-time position, with no significant differences by age, gender, or minority or SCSEP status. When asked why they were not looking for a full-time position, almost one-third responded that they would like more leisure time and one-fifth each indicated either that they or a spouse was in poor health, or that they did not want the hassle of a full-time position. Very few—about 15 percent—reported Social Security restrictions as an impediment. Again, there were no significant variations by age, gender, or minority or SCSEP status.

Qualitative Impressions about Unemployment from Some of the Unemployed and Key Agency Personnel

Impressions from the Unemployed

An example of an elder worker who wanted more free time was a 72-year-old African American male, who had been a clerk for the railroad, making $12 an hour when he left that job after 42 years in 1983. Although he got the kind of job he wanted through the placement agency, he stayed for only a month as a driver for kindergarten children—a seasonal position, where he was earning $4 an hour. When the school year ended, he decided that he wanted more free time and was not planning to look for another job any time soon. Additional leisure time was worth more to him at this point than another part-time position. He and his wife lived on about $12,000 a year, which included a small VA pension and a private pension from the railroad.

The health of a close relative was an issue for a 62-year-old African American female, who was separated and lived with her invalid mother. She had spent 30 years as a clerk in city government and "loved" the job she got from the placement agency—as an aide in a day-care center for children. She had been there only four months when her mother became incapacitated and she had to discontinue working. She had nothing but praise for the placement agency. To quote: "It's nice to know there's a place that fits one's needs and where you don't have to feel embarrassed about your age."

Another African American female, 57 years old, who had spent eight years staffing a food cart on the waterfront and had run her own catering business, also had to discontinue working because of health reasons—in this case, her own. She wanted a job as a cook, which she had gotten at a local rectory, where she remained for 12 months, earning $5 an hour. This was a very enjoyable job for her, but on the advice of her physician, she was forced to discontinue because of poor circulation in her legs. There was too much standing involved. She was eager for another position, but one that did not involve much standing. Because she was "paid under the table" in her earlier positions, she did not think she would be eligible for Social Security. She currently lived on public assistance. She indicated, upon further reflection, that not only was her health at stake in the rectory job, but she also wanted to be paid off the books, something which her employer indicated he could no longer do.

There were other unemployed elders who expressed dissatisfaction with their positions—cautiously at first, but then more directly. A white single male, aged 73, who was self-employed for 30 years as the owner of a small fabric store in South Philadelphia, wanted a job as a driver, which he secured through the placement agency. Working for a private employer, at $5 an hour, he would ferry travelers from the parking lot to the terminal at Philadelphia International Airport. However, after five months, he quit, finding the job too stressful. He was interested in another job, but was not actively searching at this point. As he put it: "At this age, you can't take any job—you can't put up with all that stuff. The fact that I was my own boss all those years may have something to do with it." He also felt there was discrimination against men in jobs for elders. He mentioned: "The clerical jobs are all for women—women have more chance for jobs than men—I look at the ads—they can't discriminate against age or sex up front, but they do."

There was another white male, aged 72, who had worked as a rigger for 28 years. He sought a driving job, which he got from the placement agency, earning $4.75 an hour. This job, which involved driving kidney patients to dialysis, required that he work three ten-hour days and be on call in the interim. When the driving company decided to dock his pay because he took a lunch hour to which he felt he was entitled, he quit. While he was somewhat lackadaisically looking for another position, his private pension of around $27,000 a year kept him comfortable enough that he didn't "have to be pushed around."

Finally, a 64-year-old white widow, who had worked for six years as an office worker 18 years ago, and had some intermittent sales-clerk positions at a large department store, wanted a general clerk position, which she secured through the placement agency and where she remained for 18 months. She liked the job at a mental health center, but the employer began to pressure her to assume a full-time position, which she did not want. As a result, she quit. She lived alone, on between $11,000 and $12,000 a year, from a combination of Social Security and a small private pension from her deceased husband's employer.

Impressions from Key Agency Personnel

First and foremost, agency personnel were not surprised that almost one-third of those whom we set out to interview were no longer working at the time of their interview. In fact, some of the key informants expressed surprise that there was not an even larger percentage unemployed. Several explanations were given—from the state of the regional economy, to unrealistic expectations on the part of some employers, and finally, to qualities of some of the elder workers themselves.

In terms of the state of the local and regional economy, there was strong recognition on the part of personnel from two of the urban placement agencies of a rather drastic downturn in the regional economy. The job market had "tightened up," especially within the previous year (1989). The private nonprofit agency personnel had seen a dramatic shift in employment trends, with fewer available jobs and an increase in elders seeking employment. This rise in the number of applicants had been especially pronounced among males. This trend was not mentioned by the key informant from the SCSEP program which placed Hispanic elders primarily, and it was only beginning to become apparent to the county placement agency, which placed both SCSEP and non-SCSEP workers.

It was actually the person responsible for job development at the county agency who reported that he was beginning to feel the constriction in the private, nonprofit sector, especially among nonservice jobs. Although county personnel did not have the impression that their clientele was getting older, when they pulled some recent agency statistics during our discussions, they found, to their surprise, that there had been a greater number of recent placements for those elders over 65 than under 65.

One informant from the urban, private, nonprofit agency also reported that it was increasingly difficult to attract foundation support. To quote: "Private foundations don't seem to view work for elders as a priority area." Likewise, another informant from the county agency anticipated that it would not be long before the effects of hiring freezes in many areas of the public sector would begin to be felt by agencies trying to place SCSEP workers.

An additional structural factor cited by one agency director was the fact that the kinds of jobs most of the elders were placed in—clerical, sales, and service jobs—were exactly the kinds of positions vulnerable to high turnover, no matter what the age of the worker. This impression is reinforced in the economic literature on part-time workers in general. Recalling Tilly's (1992a) distinction between retention and secondary part-time work, described in chapter 2, he indicated that in addition to no job ladder, and low pay, secondary part-time work was also characterized by short tenure. Drawing on Rebitzer and Taylor's work (1988), Tilly pointed out that the average job tenure for part-time workers was 3.4 years, far below the average of 8.1 years for full-time working men and 5.7 years for full-time working women. Although these data were not specific to the elderly, it is reasonable to assume that the average job tenure for older workers might well be even less than three years.

Although all of the agencies would have liked to, none was offering much in the way of training, which could extend job tenure. As mentioned previously, this general lack of training opportunities for older workers has been well documented by others (see, for example, Kuriansky and Porter forthcoming; Cox 1995; Barth, McNaught, and Rizzi 1995 and 1993). Many of the newer and more desirable clerical jobs required computer skills, which the majority of elders did not have and seemed hesitant to try to learn. As one agency informant in his forties put it: "People my age have to be retrained to work with computers and older workers require similar training." This informant also suggested that if the training was set at a slower pace, more elders might be amenable. On the other hand, the private, nonprofit-agency key informants indicated that few of their applicants were interested in a job with a lot of typing.

Even though the aim of all placement agencies was to secure permanent placements for elders, some of the available jobs were also seasonal in nature. Because of this, one key informant said: "This population drifts in and out of jobs and it's not always their fault." As mentioned previously, for some of the Hispanic elders, their occasional sporadic job attendance was often not due to the job. Rather, because about 80 percent of the Hispanic elderly served by the agency had come from Puerto Rico and liked to make frequent trips "home," it was their own personal and family schedules which were seasonal in nature, rather than a quality inherent in their part-time position.

Other jobs were not seen as very desirable by elders, like teller jobs and fast-food positions which required a lot of standing. In addition, fast-food positions often required lengthy travel and evening shifts which elders did not want. It should be noted that none of the agencies in this study did much placement with fast-food chains, largely because of their conviction that these jobs were often exploitative.

Jobs which were close to the elders' homes were clearly seen as more desirable. Likewise, as pointed out by an informant from the county agency, if the placement jobs were not close to public transportation, this would preclude a good percentage from taking the job. In addition, even though some of the more popular jobs for elder males were driving positions, if these elders needed to use their own car, the job became more difficult to fill.

Still other jobs, like companion positions and nursing-home jobs, which were more readily available, were also not seen as desirable by some elders. An informant from the county office indicated that the home-health agencies were particularly "desperate" for workers—that she could place elders immediately at $6.50 an hour at a local home for the aged, but her applicants "won't touch it." Finally there was also a conviction on the part of some agency personnel that society doesn't much care about the older worker: either what they want or what they need in terms of a job. As one staffer put it: "We have a system that does not consider the needs of the older person in general." This ambivalent attitude toward older workers has been echoed over and over again in the literature (see, for example, Barth, McNaught, and Rizzi 1995 and 1993).

Last, for some elder part-timers, unemployment resulted because of conflicts which arose on the job between the elders and their employers. According to one informant, some elders had trouble accepting criticism from employers, which he interpreted as sometimes occurring because younger workers were in supervisory roles and some elders found this difficult. Another generational difficulty that sometimes arose stemmed from the fact that some elders "have not learned how to be assertive and express their concerns—they tend to keep their feelings in, resulting in an outburst or in absenteeism," which might result in the loss of their job. In terms of this alleged generational difference in expressive style, for many of the elders, having the job was essential to quite modest economic survival, thus making the open expression of complaints both more risky and less likely.

This was a two-way street, however. According to this same informant, some employers had experienced the flip side of the same problem—namely, some employers had difficulty communicating with the older worker, especially in terms of conveying criticism. Some of these employers "have trouble understanding the issues of the older worker." Some did not have a good understanding of the physical and psychological aspects of aging, which could create difficulties for both older workers and their employers. According to this informant, while complaints were usually made informally, the most frequent ones from the employee perspective were either that "I'm not appreciated" or "there is too much work thrown at me." From the employer's perspective, most frequently voiced complaints were: "they are too slow," or the worker "isn't picking up fast enough."

Summary

The unemployed did not differ from those still employed part-time in any substantial way: neither demographically, in terms of prior work history, or the kinds of jobs they received from the placement agencies. The unemployed did, however, express more concern about their physical health, reported somewhat lower energy levels, and described themselves as somewhat more limited in the kind of work they could do. Likewise, significantly fewer of the unemployed than part-time elders reported getting the placement agency job they wanted.

For the majority, their last position had been the one secured by the placement agency, where they had worked around a year on average. The majority had been out of work about ten months, on average, at the time of the interview. There was no predominant reason reported for leaving the placement agency job. About one-fifth reported leaving because of their own poor health or that of a spouse or other relative; another one-fifth left involuntarily, because they were laid off or the job ended; about one-tenth left because they wanted to work less; a negligible percentage, because of retirement; and about one-third, because of miscellaneous reasons, including a small percentage because of job dissatisfaction.

Responses to open-ended questions indicated that there might have been more job dissatisfaction than was directly expressed. The majority of those unemployed had left the job at their own initiative and were not currently looking for another job. If and when they did, they were definitely committed to part-time employment.

Agency informants were generally not surprised by the extent of the unemployment; some were surprised that it was not even greater. They cited a range of reasons—from a downturn in the regional economy; to the high turnover in sales, clerical, and service positions, whatever the age of the worker; to differences in style between older workers and younger supervisors; and to an overall sense that society at large was not too interested in the older worker.

It seems reasonable to conclude, therefore, that a combination of characteristics of the unemployed themselves, such as poorer health and lower energy levels; characteristics of their familial and social milieu, such as the poor health of a spouse or other relative; generational misunderstandings between the elders and their employers and younger co-workers; characteristics of secondary part-time jobs in general, which typically have a short job tenure; and characteristics of the local and regional economy, all contributed to elder-worker unemployment. No single factor was predominant.

While the literature has documented the fact that unemployment rates are lower for workers 65 and older than for younger workers, it has also repeatedly documented that older workers are more likely to become unemployed as a result of job loss and to experience greater difficulties in obtaining re-employment when they lose their jobs (Kuriansky and Porter forthcoming; Sum and Fogg 1990; National Commission on Working Women 1987; 9 to 5 1987, 1986).

Likewise, although not expressed directly by most of the unemployed respondents, the role that worker discouragement played in their not seeking another job cannot be ruled out by our data. Worker discouragement is regarded by many experts as an extremely prevalent and somewhat intractable problem for elderly workers—one that only worsens with age (Kuriansky and Porter forthcoming; Bales 1989; National Commission on Working Women 1987; 9 to 5 1987). The fact that there was some dissatisfaction expressed about the kinds of positions obtained, especially by some of the unemployed whose financial circumstances were somewhat more secure, is also suggestive. For this subgroup, the kinds of jobs obtained were not judged to be worth the effort.

What we do know is that the majority of the respondents in our study—both employed and unemployed—had incomes hovering near or below the poverty line. The fact that re-employment for elders is difficult heightens concern about their even greater economic vulnerability in the future.

Chapter Thirteen
The Special Case of the Full-Time Employed

This chapter briefly describes the demographic characteristics of the full-time employed, their most important reasons for applying to the job-placement agency, and the kinds of work they were performing. The chapter ends by comparing their fringe benefits and attitudes toward work and retirement with those of the part-time employed. The basic questions addressed are whether and in what ways the full-time elder workers differed from those working part-time. Because only 21 elders were working full-time when interviewed, results should be interpreted cautiously.

Demographic Characteristics

Of the 21 full-time employed elders, who represented 8 percent of all elders interviewed, 15 were female and 6 were male. In terms of marital status and current living arrangements, the full-timers were also reasonably similar to the part-timers. Eight were married, six were widowed, five were divorced, and two were single. Of the eight who were married, four had spouses who were still working; four had spouses who were no longer employed. Slightly less than half (10) of the full-timers lived alone. In spite of their working full-time, finances were still limited. Although somewhat more of the full-timers than part-timers (38 percent vs. 24 percent) had household incomes of more than $15,000 per year, it was rather startling to note that five of the full-timers had incomes of less than $7,000 per year. This was also in spite of the fact that the full-timers had somewhat more education than the part-timers. Almost half of the full-timers had some education beyond high school, whereas only about one-quarter of the part-timers did. Likewise, a somewhat larger proportion of the full- than part-timers were white: ten were white, ten were African American, and one was Hispanic.

There were several additional areas where the full-timers and part-timers differed, all of which might have contributed to the differences in current work status. First, the full-timers, on average, were younger than the part-timers. While the mean age of the full-timers was 64 years, the mean age of the part-timers was 67 years. While about two-thirds of the part-timers were over 65, slightly less than half of the full-timers were.

Likewise, there were clear differences in health status. While somewhat over one-quarter of the part-timers reported having significant health difficulties, none of the full-timers did. Neither the amount of worry their health had caused them nor their level of energy relative to their peers were different for full-timers than part-timers, although scores for full-timers tended to be higher (e.g., less worry and more energy). However, there were differences between the two groups in terms of their assessment of their personal health relative to their peers. On a four-point scale (where 1 = fair, 2 = poor, 3 = good, and 4 = excellent) the mean for the full-timers was 3.5, compared to a mean of 3.2 for the part-timers. Overall, then, the full-timers reported being in somewhat better health than the part-timers.

Reasons for Applying to the Job-Placement Agency

More of the part-timers had actually been seeking a part-time job when they came to the placement agency: about four-fifths of the part-timers, compared to about half of the full-timers. On the other hand, one-quarter of the full-timers had definitely wanted a full-time job, compared to a negligible percentage of the part-timers. The remaining full-timers indicated that either a part- or full-time job was acceptable. The response by full-timers to this question is also consistent with the full-timers' lower rating of the importance of working part-time as a reason for their first applying to the placement agency. While this was the second most important reason for the part-timers' applying, with a mean rating of 3.5 (between "somewhat" and "very important"), the average mean rating for this item for the full-timers was 2.8 (between "not very important" and "somewhat important") and was fifth in terms of their overall item rankings.

The items receiving the highest ratings for the full-timers were (in descending order): (1) "needed the money"; (2) "working close to home"; (3) "to keep busy"; and (4) "help others."

Current Position

One full-timer was in a professional or managerial position, 11 were in clerical and/or sales positions, seven were in service positions, and two were in unspecified kinds of positions. On average, these elders worked 37 hours a week, having worked in their current position an average of one year. Although all of the placement agencies involved in the study made some full-time job placements, only about one-third of the full-timers got their position through the agency. On average, full-time elder workers were making $6.97 an hour, higher than the average hourly wage ($4.78) of the part-timers.

Fringe Benefits

In order to assess the range and quantity of fringe benefits received by the full-timers, the Full-Time Fringe Benefits Index, developed by Quinn and Staines (1979), was used. Using the identical items and scoring as the Part-Time Fringe Benefit Index, presented in Table 5 in chapter 7, this index had good internal reliability (alpha = 0.77). The index mean and standard deviation were 0.33 and 0.21, with a potential score range of 0 to 1. As has been well documented in the literature (Saltford and Snider 1994; Golden 1992; Kahne 1992; Blank 1990; 9 to 5 1986), full-timers in the study received more fringe benefits than the part-timers overall.

Looking first at health benefits and pension coverage, the two private-employee benefits which constituted the largest dollar expenditures in 1985 (Woodbury 1989), three-quarters of all full-time workers in this country received health-insurance coverage through employers, and over one-half received pension coverage (Levitan and Conway 1988). As expected, benefit coverage was uneven across work sectors. Among those industries with low benefit/wage ratios were the service and retail trade industries (Mitchell 1988), where the majority of all of the elder workers in this study were employed. There were also differences in coverage by gender. Drawing upon Current Population Survey data for 1987, Blank (1990) reported that overall, 74 percent of workers who were female heads of households, 60 percent of workers who were wives, and 79 percent of male workers received health benefits. In our sample, 65 percent of full-time workers were covered, which does not compare too badly with figures from the Current Population Survey for 1987.

Referring again to Blank's (1990) findings for 1987, 50 percent of all female workers who were heads of households received pension coverage, while 51 percent of all workers who were wives and 58.5 percent of all male workers were covered. In our sample, about one-third of elder full-time employees were covered, which is not as good a showing overall as for the health-benefit category.

Close to three-quarters of the full-timers received paid vacations and holidays, while slightly less than one-half received sick leave with full pay and life insurance.

Attitudes toward Work and Retirement

Using the same set of items used in Table 10 in chapter 11 to gauge the attitudes of part-timers toward work and retirement, the full-timers' views were also assessed. Some interesting differences emerged between the two groups of elder workers. While the part-timers rated all of the work-attitude items (items 4–7 in Table 10) in the "agree" range, with item 7—about the importance of promotions—receiving the highest rating, the means for the full-timers on these items were somewhat lower and all at the top of the "disagree" range (e.g., #4—"Work is the most meaningful part of life" (x = 3.0); #5—"Most people think more of someone who works than they do of someone who doesn't" (x = 2.9); #6—"A good secure income is more important than getting raises" (x = 2.86); and #7—"A chance for promotion is an important part of any good job" (x = 2.90).

Considering the first three items in Table 10, all of which related to retirement attitudes, the comparison with the part-timers was again instructive. While both the full-timers and part-timers had moderate views of the attractiveness of retirement, with the ratings for both groups of elders on these items in the "disagree" range, all three items were rated more negatively by the full-timers than by the part-timers. As was true for the part-timers, full-timers were least likely to agree that "older workers should retire in order to give younger people more of a chance on the job." Overall, then, the full-timers did not see retirement as something to look forward to, nor did they feel they should step aside so that younger workers could have more chances on the job.

Summary

In terms of demographic characteristics, the full-timers were reasonably similar to the part-timers in terms of gender (the majority were female), marital status (more were widowed, divorced, or single than married), and current living arrangement (close to half from each group lived alone). Somewhat more of the full-timers had household incomes of $15,000 and over. Full-timers did have somewhat more education—with close to half compared to one-quarter of the part-timers with education beyond high school. Likewise, almost half of the full-timers, compared to one-third of the part-timers, were white. The full-timers were also younger; while half of the full-timers were under 65, the majority of the part-timers were over 65. Finally, while none of the full-timers reported having any significant health difficulties, close to one-third of the part-timers did. Full-timers also reported themselves as being in better health, comparable to their same-aged peers, than did the part-timers.

More of the full-timers than part-timers had been looking for a full-time job when they first came to the job-placement agency. They also rated items having to do with "needing the money" and "working close to home" as more important than "keeping busy" and "wanting to work part-time"—the two most important reasons for the part-timers approaching the job-placement agency. While the majority of the part-timers were still in the jobs the placement agencies had secured for them, only about one-third of the full-timers were. However, the kinds of jobs the full-timers were working in were similar to those of the part-timers, with a heavy concentration in clerical and/or sales or service positions.

As expected, full-timers did receive proportionately more fringe benefits than the part-timers, though somewhat fewer of them received health insurance and pension coverage than did other American workers during the same time period. Close to three-quarters of them did receive paid vacations and holidays, while slightly less than one-half received sick leave with full pay and life insurance.

When their attitudes toward work and retirement were compared with those of the part-timers, the full-timers reported somewhat less commitment to the work ethic and even more negative attitudes about retirement. Their lower commitment to the work ethic is somewhat puzzling. Because data were not collected about the full-timers' levels of job satisfaction or other indicators of job quality discussed in chapter 9, we do not know whether their jobs were less satisfying overall than were those of the part-timers. It is certainly a possibility. We also do not know whether they would have preferred to be working less. However, we do know that in spite of the fact that they were younger, had more education, and perceived themselves to be in better health than the part-timers, their total household income did not differ appreciably from that of the part-timers, a clear indicator that economic need and vulnerability remained important, even for those with full-time positions. These questions obviously require further study, with a larger comparison group of lower-income elder workers who are employed full-time.

Chapter Fourteen
Conclusions and Recommendations

Introduction

Few would disagree that older Americans have been subject to greater scrutiny in recent years. The rapidly expanding number of persons surviving into old age has been accompanied by increasing interest in their economic, social, and psychological well-being by researchers, policymakers, program planners, the media, and even the general public. Such interest will only increase as the baby-boom generation moves into old age during the next quarter of a century.

Further, there is evidence of increased concern about the adequacy of retirement resources for baby-boomers and others across the life span and social-class spectrum. Given the current national debate over entitlement programs, there are sound reasons for anticipating future reductions in benefit levels for Medicare, Medicaid, and Social Security, all programs which, until recently, seemed reasonably secure. Clearly many Americans, including the majority of our respondents, do not anticipate retirement as a relaxed or pleasant time of life, but rather one likely to include significant financial anxiety.

The anticipated need for many elders to work well into old age is therefore a response not only to the desires of many older citizens to remain productive, but also to their need to acquire the resources necessary to maintain financial independence and a reasonable level of subsistence. Contrary to the popular notion of older people as a "leisured class" (Carnevale and Stone 1994, p. 101), about 12 percent of elders 65 and over currently live in poverty. This group includes many women, living alone, and elders of color, groups expected to expand in the future and the subjects of our research investigation.

Part-time employment represents the most popular alternative work option for older persons, yet one about which we are just beginning to have systematic empirical data. Even though surveys of older workers over the last fifteen years have consistently reported elders' preferences for part-time work, we have amazingly little empirical data assessing their lived experience of this work option. Does the reality of available part-time work match elders' expressed desires for, and expectations about, this work option?

These are important considerations, given the fact that part-time employment has always been a controversial work arrangement—one that has grown only more so in the last five to ten years. While voluntary part-time work has expanded, so too has involuntary part-time work, leading some economists to interpret this growth as a barometer of negative and perhaps permanent change in the world of work and a widening insecurity in the economy as a whole. Further, negative stereotypes about part-time workers as second-class workers have persisted. In spite of ample evidence to the contrary, many part-time employees continue to be characterized as less committed, productive, and dependable than their full-time counterparts, even though there is no empirical evidence to support these claims.

There are examples of "good" part-time work—with fringe benefits and wages prorated to those of equivalent full-time jobs, with secure job attachment, career potential, and ongoing opportunities for job training—but the reality is that much part-time work today is "bad" or secondary part-time work, with insecure job attachment and high turnover; little or no opportunity for career advancement and additional training; low productivity; low wages, with few or no fringe benefits; and concentrated in the low-paid retail and service sectors, where future job expansion is most likely to occur. Like other kinds of alternative work arrangements, including working off-the-books and temporary-help services, secondary part-time employment typically falls under the rubric of contingent work.

Even though the numbers of all workers employed part-time expanded by about 90 percent in the last 25 years, its growth as a percentage of the total work force during these same years was minimal—about 3 percent (Saltford and Snider 1994). However, for those 55 and over, the incidence of part-time work increases with age. At the same time that the overall labor force participation rates for white males 55 and over have plummeted, there is also recent evidence of increasing participation in part-time work by workers 55 and older. The expansion in the part-time work sector for older workers, like the demographics of aging, may serve to bring this phenomenon to the attention of the professional and lay public with increased frequency in the years ahead. Our research was a beginning response to this need.

As a form of employment, we know that part-time work is concentrated among three major groups in society: younger workers; female workers, especially those with dependents at home; and older workers. These three groups are not homogenous with respect to reasons for seeking and maintaining part-time employment. As Christiansen (1990) pointed out:

Older workers are not fungible with teenage workers. Government and business should be cautious about treating older workers as they do teenage workers. Although the fast-food and child care industries have turned to older workers to offset the severe labor shortages caused by the shrinking cohort of young workers, any large-scale effort to substitute older workers for teenage ones should not be promoted unless several conditions are met. Older workers want respect, dignity, and appreciation for a lifetime of work. They do not want to be seen as just bodies. A teenager may take a job to fill time, but an older worker uses a job to organize time. Older workers want to be appreciated for the time they spend. The extent to which they might trade off earnings for appreciation is not entirely clear. . . . (p. 203)

We also know that older part-time workers are not homogeneous either. While there may be some similar reasons for all elders seeking and maintaining part-time employment, we also expect there to be differences as well, which need further exploration.

As pointed out by Christensen, Axel, Hewitt, and Nardone (1992), older part-time employees can be divided into several categories. The first category includes retirees, who generally have a pension, health benefits in many cases, and possibly some savings. This group is typically either self-employed or working part-time because they want to supplement their retirement income or don't want to stop working entirely. As pointed out by Doeringer (1990b), this is also the group for whom part-time work can provide a bridging function between career employment and final retirement. While this group is not limited to males, most of the recent empirical investigations of this group have included only males.

The second group, who are typically male, white collar, and well educated, are middle managers who have been forced out of their jobs because of downsizing. For this group, part-time work is typically involuntary—because they cannot find a full-time job.

The third group are chronic contingent workers, with limited safety nets, who have spent their worklife in semiskilled and unskilled jobs, primarily in retail sales or the service sector. This is an understudied group and one that includes most of the elder workers in our study. This is not a group for whom part-time work provides a bridge to retirement. Rather it is a group which includes some elders who may well have to "work till they die."

Indeed, it was the continuing lack of attention accorded this group of older persons which served as an incentive to us to undertake our research. Specifically, inadequate attention has been focused on the experience of low-income older adults, particularly those committed to continuing to engage in modified levels of gainful employment in their later years. Not only have low-income older workers as a group been neglected, but so also have older women and elders from racial and other minority groups who have chosen to re-enter America's workplace on a part-time basis.

Low-income, part-time employed older adults have remained relatively well-insulated from the plethora of manpower, training, and employment studies carried out in the past. Perhaps this is because they have not been seen as a particularly glamorous or influential group, either among the elderly or among the employed. As a result, such issues as their job commitment and satisfaction; workplace expectations; experiences with job-placement programs; relationships with same-aged and younger co-workers; and perceived discrimination on the basis of age, gender, and race/ethnicity are not well understood.

The major intent of this research was to better understand the experience of part-time employment, from the low-income, elder worker's perspective. It was hoped that this research would provide a rarely heard voice from this group of vulnerable elders. Did part-time work serve primarily an instrumental function, enabling older adults to secure those desperately needed additional dollars which made life somewhat more manageable? What other functions did these jobs serve for this group of workers? Given current perspectives on job quality, were the part-time jobs our study respondents received mostly "good" or mostly "bad" part-time jobs? How did our respondents evaluate these jobs—as mostly good or mostly bad? Did they experience discrimination at work, based on age, gender, race/ethnicity, or because they worked part-time? These are among the questions we explored.

There are several limitations to this study. Our research was restricted to the experience of a select group of elder part-timers in the greater Philadelphia metropolitan area, interviewed in late 1989 and early 1990. Some observers might consider this to be an "aging" data base, not reflective of current trends and developments in the work-force attachments of older workers. However, we argue that the conditions of employment for low-income elder part-time employees have not changed significantly since the late 1980s, but, in fact, may have even deteriorated somewhat since then. We know, for example, that SCSEP programs nationwide are subject to the same budget reductions facing other federal programs (Deets 1995; Lehrmann 1995). Consequently, our data remain a useful barometer of the employment experiences of low-income elders, with jobs secured by private nonprofit and publicly funded job-placement programs in both the private and public sectors. Our results, of course, cannot speak to the unknown quantity of elder workers who seek jobs on their own, without the assistance of a job-placement program.

Further, while not true for the nation as a whole, almost all of the elders in the three SCSEP programs in our study were placed in subsidized positions. In addition, comparative analysis of the demographic profiles of our study's SCSEP participants with SCSEP participants nationwide confirmed similar distributions for gender, age, and education. However, unlike SCSEP programs in the aggregate nationwide, our sample purposely included a larger percentage of minorities. Generalizations are therefore limited to this particular study sample.

However, at the very least, results of this exploratory/descriptive study provide a rich and full account of a variety of facets of the part-time work experience for a group of employees whose experience of re-entry into the low-wage, semiskilled and unskilled sector of the work force has gone largely unnoticed in the academic literature and in the popular press. These workers do not include the high-profile, professional employee occasionally featured in news accounts of elder citizens who have either returned to work or never left the labor force. Rather, the low-income, mostly minority workers in our research were by and large ordinary citizens, with financial resources in many cases insufficient to lift them to or above the poverty threshold even in the presence of part-time employment.

Conclusions
a. "Good Jobs"/"Bad Jobs"

Drawing upon our interpretive framework presented in chapter 2, we first address the issue of wages and the receipt of fringe benefits. From this standpoint, the jobs our respondents obtained were mostly "bad" contingent part-time jobs. While above the minimum wage for 1985, the median hourly wage for study elders of $4.78 an hour was somewhat lower than median hourly wages reported for all part-time workers in 1985, and moderately lower than mean hourly wages for all part-time workers, based on 1987 Current Population Survey figures. Even with the income from their part-time jobs, the majority of our respondents remained poor, with a marginal standard of living.

Further, when elders worked overtime, they received either no compensation or were paid their regular hourly wage, both clearly exploitative practices. Elders also received few fringe benefits. While our respondents would have preferred more fringe benefits, especially the more costly health and retirement benefits, they did not expect them and were quite pragmatic and realistic in their appraisal, a point which Sterns and Miklos (1995) have also made about older workers.

However, if we examine some of the nonwage benefits, or "compensating differentials," our respondents reported, the evaluation of their part-time jobs definitely tips in the positive direction, even though these jobs were poorly paid and provided minimum fringe benefits.

First, for almost three-fourths of our elder workers, their jobs were voluntary part-time positions, in the service, sales, and clerical sectors, where they had also held their career positions. They were seeking part-time work and that is what they got. The majority also received the kind of position they were looking for when they first went to the job-placement agency. Their three major reasons for initial application to the job-placement agency were to keep busy, to obtain a part-time job, and because they needed the money. The first and third reasons coincide with the first two functions of work, described by Friedmann and Havighurst (1954)—income or financial return and work as a regulator of life activity, providing order and routine to life.

Further, based on their experience on the job, the majority said that if they had it to do over again, they would take the same job again without hesitation. Over three-quarters of their positions were judged to be steady, nonseasonal jobs, certainly one indicator of job security. Almost 80 percent of the jobs were judged to have predictable hours, not subject to the whims of their employers. Almost 80 percent of the elders worked the same days and hours each week and expressed satisfaction with their schedules. On the other hand, while few saw any difficulty in taking time off occasionally to take care of personal or family matters, they felt, as a whole, that it would not be easy to change their work schedule on a permanent basis.

In addition, the majority reported using existing skills and acquiring new skills on the job. Unfortunately, we did not probe the specifics of these new or existing skills. Close to two-thirds of our respondents indicated that they worked with, and enjoyed working with, other same-aged, part-time workers. There were also many opportunities to work with younger workers, which they reported enjoying, even though there was some anecdotal evidence from the elders and from agency informants to the contrary. It should be noted that opportunities to work with other part-time employees, both younger and older, provided a supportive work context and was one important factor that mitigated against reports of feeling peripheral on the job.

Many part-time employees, particularly younger professional women with young children at home, often find themselves in work situations where they are isolated, being the only one or one of very few part-time employees in a particular work unit. Among other factors, this structural isolation can make them feel more peripheral on the job (Barker 1993). However, for our respondents, both intergenerational and intragenerational interaction, as well as inter-action with other part-time employees, was a common experience, one that these elders generally much appreciated.

In addition, these elders were quite sociable, reporting not only high levels of contact with their relatives and friends off the job, but significant friendly and supportive interactions at work. Their ex-tensive social contacts at work coincided with two of Friedmann and Havighurst's (1954) functions of work: (1) developing mean-ingful social relationships and (2) having meaningful life experiences.

Therefore, part-time work served multiple functions for these elders. It not only provided a crucial supplement to their limited finances, but also served as a vehicle for connection with others and as a way of remaining vital. Clearly both economic and social needs were being satisfied through employment, with one appearing no less important than the other.

Elders reported high levels of commitment to their jobs and to the work ethic, as well as strongly positive overall job satisfaction. Items having to do with reasonable physical surroundings, the ca-pacity of supervisors to get people to work together, and co-workers taking a personal interest in them were all rated quite positively. While we did not ask directly about the extent of hazardous expo-sure at work, this is a condition that would undoubtedly have sur-faced, if such were the case. And they did report satisfaction with their physical surroundings at work.

Likewise, we can assume that the level of physical exertion was acceptable to them and was something agency personnel kept in mind when making placements. Very few placements were made either in nursing homes or fast-food establishments because of the levels of physical exertion required—either heavy lifting, having to stand up for long periods of time, or having to work at a continuous fast pace.

We conclude that at least for these elders, there were definite nonwage benefits or "compensating differentials" in their part-time jobs, which offset to some degree their low wages and minimal fringe benefits. While these compensating differentials might not have been acceptable to the two other groups of elder part-time workers referred to previously, or to other categories of part-time workers, including youth or women with young dependents, they seemed acceptable to the elders in our study who were still working part-time when interviewed.

At the same time, we are mindful of Tilly's (1996) suggestion that

> . . . *according to the psychological theory of cognitive dissonance, people who find themselves in a situation that goes against their prior preferences will in many cases change their preferences. In other words, people will rationalize their situation* post hoc—*for example, some involuntary part-time workers will convince themselves that they actually prefer part-time hours. (p. 7)*

However, given the number of favorable job components reported by our respondents, we do not believe that these positive characterizations can be dismissed as mere rationalizations. From the perspective of our respondents, their jobs were basically "good" part-time jobs. Further, as Friedman (1992) has stated:

> . . . *the distinction between good and bad jobs is not clear, particularly for mature workers. Whether a job is good or bad depends not only on the characteristics of the job, but also on the needs of the workers. The "good" high-skills jobs appeal to some, but may not be suitable for all older workers. On the other hand, a temporary or part-time job might provide a desired degree of flexibility for some mature workers, and even low-paying jobs might be attractive to those who want to stay below Social Security earning limits. In other words, the whole range of job types may provide opportunities to older workers. (pp. 54–55)*

Or put another way, the old adage that "one man's meat is another man's poison" seems particularly applicable here.

b. Discrimination in Part-Time Elder Employment

There was some discrepancy between the findings from our discrimination indices, which indicated almost no reported discrimination on the basis of age, gender, race/ethnicity, or part-time work status, and the passing remarks of some elders and key informants who indicated that such discrimination, especially that based on age and race/ethnicity, did exist at work for some of the elders (Kaye and Alexander 1995). Nonetheless, such occurrences were not judged to be significant problems at work and were often subtle, as the literature has documented.

On the other hand, there seemed little question that the placement agencies served as buffers against age and gender discrimination, at least at the time of initial hiring. Agency informants and elders provided numerous anecdotal accounts of this buffering effect. Further, because of well-documented age discrimination in the workplace, it seems doubtful that the majority of our respondents would have secured these jobs without the assistance of the placement agency, a point made again and again by our respondents.

At the same time, perhaps discrimination was simply less apparent in the roughly 50 percent of placements that were subsidized. In these cases, there may have been little reason for employers to discriminate, since they did not have to pay the employees from their own payroll. It may also be, as Henretta (1994) suggested, that overt discrimination was not a major issue because part-time and temporary jobs "are not entry portals to careers carrying fringe benefits, training, and job commitment" (p. 75).

c. Turnover in Part-Time Employment

A somewhat unexpected finding, at least to us, was the relatively high rate of unemployment—about 30 percent—only two years postplacement. As reviewed in chapter 12, part-timers and those unemployed had largely similar demographic profiles, except for the following: the unemployed did not perceive themselves to be as healthy, to have as high energy levels, and saw themselves as somewhat more limited in the kind of work they could do than their part-time counterparts. Both groups of elders had considerable previous work experience and sought part-time positions voluntarily, primarily to keep busy and to secure additional income.

For the majority of the unemployed elders, no single predominant reason was provided for their leaving the placement job. However, there were two areas where part-timers and unemployed elders disagreed. First, significantly more of the part-time than the unemployed elders got the job they had in mind when they first went to the job-placement agency. And second, some unemployed elders reported varying degrees of job dissatisfaction. It is possible that the unemployeds' reports of poorer health might have seemed to them to be more socially acceptable justifications for not working than acknowledging job dissatisfaction. Since we had no independent indicators of health status, this is only speculation. Or perhaps for this group of elders, the kinds of jobs they obtained might simply not have been worth the effort to them.

Agency informants were generally not surprised by the 30 percent unemployment rate two years post–job-placement. To the contrary, some were surprised that more of the elders were not unemployed. Based on all the evidence we obtained from the unemployed elders, as well as from agency personnel, we conclude that there were probably a number of potential factors at play, accounting for the relatively high rate of unemployment, including: (1) factors having to do with the workers themselves, including somewhat poorer health and lower energy levels; (2) some generational misunderstandings between the elders and their employers and younger co-workers; (3) characteristics of their social and familial milieu, including the poor health of a spouse or other relative; (4) characteristics of secondary part-time jobs in general, which, according to Tilly (1992b), often have a shorter job tenure (around 3.4 years) than that of full-time positions (around 5.7 years); and (5) characteristics of the local and regional economy.

As indicated in chapter 2, we know that part-time workers as a group are more vulnerable to periods of unemployment than their full-time counterparts (Saltford and Snider 1994). We also know from the literature that older workers, once unemployed, experience greater difficulties than younger workers becoming employed again. Further, we do not know what role worker discouragement played in the unemployed elders not having sought jobs since vacating their placement positions. However, we know from the literature that worker discouragement is an extremely prevalent and somewhat intractable problem for elder workers, which only worsens with age.

While we indicated above that those elders working part-time reported some sense of job security—a characteristic of "good" part-

time jobs—they had been in their positions only about two years
when interviewed. Whether they were still in those same jobs several years later is unknown. And if they were not, and their health
had not deteriorated, we should be concerned about the level of job
security their part-time positions could provide, especially those positions that were unsubsidized. As just mentioned, we know that
part-time jobs in general are more vulnerable to periods of unemployment than full-time jobs.

Further, we do not know whether unions existed at any of the
elders' job sites. Although unionization of contingent workers has
been a contested area, both for unions and for employers, this is a
sector of the work force where union recruitment drives are anticipated to increase in the future (Carre, duRivage, and Tilly 1995).
How this will play out for part-time employees, who have typically
lacked union protection, and older part-time employees remains to
be seen.

d. Differences in the Experience of Part-Time Employment by Age, Gender, Race/Ethnicity, and SCSEP Status

There were very few instances where age per se was a significant
factor in the experience of part-time employment. In other words,
employers who were willing to employ older adults did not appear
to make distinctions between the relative merits of hiring, for example, a 62-, a 67-, or a 72-year-old, at least not according to the
self-reports of the elders we surveyed or the impressions of agency
personnel with whom we spoke.

Though perhaps somewhat surprising, gender also did not prove
to be a particularly influential variable in the part-time work experience of these elders. While there were the expected demographic
differences (women were somewhat poorer, more likely to live alone,
and more likely to be SCSEP enrollees), both men and women reported roughly similar levels of the following: education, health, satisfaction with their way of living, overall happiness, and receipt of
pensions, Social Security, and Medicare.

The longest or career position for both men and women had
been full-time, with an average job tenure of about twenty years.
The females in our study were not displaced homemakers; all had
extensive work histories. Men and women also reported similar rea-

sons for applying to the job-placement agencies and received similar levels of fringe benefits. Although average salaries were somewhat higher for men, the differences were not statistically significant. Men and women also reported similar assessments of overall job quality, including similar levels of job commitment and satisfaction with the part-time work experience. Women, however, did report longer periods of unemployment than men, a factor well documented in the literature on older women workers.

Regarding differences by race/ethnicity, whites were better-off financially than either Hispanics or African Americans. Almost two-thirds of the Hispanics and African Americans had incomes less than $10,000 per year, while the majority of whites had incomes over $10,000 per year. More of the Hispanics reported health problems than African Americans or whites, and had significantly less education. Almost 75 percent of the Hispanics had less than an eighth-grade education and had experienced more periods of unemployment over their work lives.

While SCSEP enrollees earned somewhat less than non-SCSEP enrollees, they did receive somewhat better fringe benefits than non-SCSEP enrollees. In addition to the annual physical and Workmen's Compensation which are required by SCSEP programs nationwide, two of the study SCSEP programs required some paid sick leave, paid vacation time, and paid holidays. SCSEP enrollees reported somewhat more interaction with co-workers and reported learning more new skills on the job. On the other hand, SCSEP enrollees as a group were less skilled to begin with than non-SCSEP workers.

e. Job Placement Programs and the Low-Income Elderly

While we did not intend through our research to evaluate the efficacy of the job training and placement programs that participated in this study, we should indicate our perspective on the relative value of these programs. As noted earlier, most of our elder respondents indicated consistently high levels of satisfaction with the performance of their job-placement agency.

There seems little question that job-placement programs, whether private nonprofit or SCSEP programs, played an important protective role in the job-seeking experience of these elders. The screening function of the job-placement program generally provided an acceptable match between the employer and employee. SCSEP programs, in particular, generally provided more fringe benefits, though some of the most desired benefits, such as health insurance and retirement benefits, were not provided.

The one area where the SCSEP programs in our study were not effective was in providing unsubsidized placements. Only a handful of our SCSEP respondents were placed in unsubsized placements, compared to about 22 percent of SCSEP enrollees nationwide in fiscal 1987. At the same time, our SCSEP sample had far more minority participants than the SCSEP program nationwide, with a high percentage of one minority—Hispanics—having less than an eighth-grade education. Further, there was some evidence that the SCSEP program serving mostly Hispanics at times assumed a paternalistic and somewhat infantalizing orientation when assessing elder workers' ability and their capacity to maneuver workplace complexities on their own in a successful fashion.

Although job training for elders in general is abysmal in this country, we are concerned that none of the programs in our study offered much in the way of formal training or retooling. Given the dramatic escalation in the use of computers and other related technology in all levels of employment, it is difficult to justify the absence of such preparatory skills-building as part of a well-balanced package of services made available to older job seekers.

Recommendations for the Future

On the one hand, we agree with Steven Sandell, who argued in 1988 that subsidized employment was an important component of employment policy for persons with short work horizons. At the same time, given the meager financial resources of the majority of our study participants, many of these workers will need to continue to work for more than the short-term, if they are to manage financially. While we applaud the desire to work and the productivity of older workers, especially when they are relatively healthy, as our respondents were, we would also agree with Martha Holstein (1992) and others who caution that too much emphasis on the productive capacities of the "healthy old" could rather easily translate "opportunities to work into expectations to work in whatever jobs become available" (p. 27). Older people should not have to "work till they die," unless they so choose. Because of the fragile state of their finances, complete retirement was not a viable option for the majority of our respondents.

There is no question that low-income elders who want to work part-time can greatly benefit from the services of a job-placement program geared to older workers. Further, without subsidized employment, a sizable number of older job seekers would not secure employment, and in turn, would never be considered by employers who have unsubsidized positions. However, from what agency personnel described, it was also apparent that many older workers were not being hired by non-SCSEP employers because many remained largely unskilled and were, at the same time, able to continue for extended periods of time as subsidized employees.

Without more comprehensive and extended training, older adults may either remain in subsidized jobs or drop out and leave the work force altogether, joining the ranks of the unemployed. This is a worrisome outcome, given the marginal incomes of many of these workers and the fact that re-employment is often quite difficult for unemployed elders.

Some employers who utilized older part-time workers in subsidized placements seemed to view such individuals, not as legitimate and valued employees, but rather as "free labor." Subsidized employment, while serving to protect the older adult from certain dangers within the work environment, does not necessarily encourage employer commitment to an eventual unsubsidized position for those individuals placed in subsidized positions in their businesses and organizations.

The benefits of subsidized employment notwithstanding, this type of program may tend to undermine the value of older workers by inadvertently sending out the wrong message, i.e., that the employer is doing the job-placement program a "favor" by creating a position for the older person. According to agency key informants, some employers underestimated the value of the older worker because they were not paying for the service and thus had less at stake. From this perspective, subsidized employment may be perpetuating the myth that older workers are incapable of being productive in the workplace.

Given the scenario just described, the following recommendations are offered:

1. Both SCSEP and non-SCSEP employment programs should consider a heightened focus on training and retraining older workers, rather than placing them in jobs solely as a means of providing them with supplemental income. Added income, while a crucial aspect of job placement for this cohort of elderly job seekers, should not be the sole focus of agency efforts. In particular, Hispanic older workers in our sample were greatly lacking in job skills, in addition to English-language skills. Taken together, these factors serve to severely inhibit their ability to obtain unsubsidized positions. While satisfied with the jobs they received, these elders may remain largely dependent on the job-placement program and the subsidization process.

Because a sizable number of older, low-income workers may wish jobs in clerical fields, and because of the recent dramatic escalation in the use of computers and related technology in virtually all fields and all levels of employment, training in this area is essential if older workers are to be able to get jobs and perform well once they get them.

2. SCSEP and non-SCSEP placement programs should consider further formalizing their evaluation process of employee/employer experiences. Additional follow-up by placement personnel seems needed. Once placed in positions, and in the absence of adequate evaluative instruments, a number of older workers have the potential of "slipping through the cracks." Consequently, the reasons employees leave their jobs become difficult, if not impossible, to assess accurately.

3. Employers in both the public and private sectors need continued encouragement to hire older workers. The incentive of subsidization is helpful in this respect, but in and of itself does not guarantee a decent and successful work experience. Employers, in exchange for benefiting from a subsidized work force, need to be encouraged to assume an accommodating posture. They need to be further sensitized to the aging process, to creative scheduling, and to building in longer-term work and training opportunities for the older part-time employee.

4. In similar fashion, older workers need to be more educated consumers in terms of their job-seeking behaviors. Instead of being timid and grateful for their employment opportunities, they need to

present themselves as the experienced, dependable, and hard-working individuals they are. To this end, placement agencies might ask selective elder workers whose placement experiences have resulted in particularly fortuitous matches to speak on a rotating basis to groups of elders who have recently sought jobs from their agencies. Furthermore, national organizations which advocate specifically for older workers should be encouraged to address the special needs of older low-income part-time employees.

5. Both elders and placement personnel should take seriously the notion that even though these part-time jobs are typically located in a secondary labor market, one characterized by low wages, poor benefits, little chance for promotion, and fragile job security, there can, at the same time, be positives associated with these positions. Most discussions about part-time positions are usually limited to the positives associated with the greater flexibility afforded by such work options.

However, as revealed in this study, when these jobs are coupled with a job-placement program which promotes permanent rather than temporary placements, one of the major negatives usually associated with contingent work arrangements and jobs in the secondary labor market is minimized. Likewise, although opportunities for promotions were almost nonexistent among study respondents, this does not mean that new skills were not acquired by many elders. It should also be noted that in contrast to other groups of part-timers, especially highly educated younger part-time working women, most of our respondents were not concerned about the career potential of their part-time positions. While younger part-time workers—predominantly working mothers in professional, technical, or managerial positions—are eager to maintain skills and remain "on track" career-wise, this was minimally important for study elders.

6. When knowledge about the trade-offs associated with low-wage jobs with few fringe benefits are coupled with recent discussions of an expanded view of job quality—one not limited just to good wages and fringe benefits—the potential for manipulating the margins to the elder worker's advantage becomes a real possibility. While wages and fringe benefits were meager, there were nonwage benefits or "compensating differentials," which were highly attractive to elder workers in this study, ones which should be highlighted

and assessed in making the decision to pursue a placement position by agency personnel and the decision to accept a position by elder workers. These include such factors as the predictability of hours and potential for some schedule flexibility; the opportunity to use existing skills and learn some new ones; and the opportunity to keep busy and have social stimulation, including the chance to work with other same-age peers who are employed part-time.

7.   If they have not done so already, placement personnel should become familiar with the kinds of information and training provided by existing organizations concerned with the promotion and improvement of alternative work schedules in general, and those dealing specifically with older workers. For part-time workers in the aggregate, such organizations include Catalyst, 9 to 5, New Ways to Work, and the Association of Part-Time Professionals. Those dealing specifically with older workers include the American Association of Retired Persons, Older Women's League, Displaced Homemakers' Network, National Caucus and Center on Black Aged, National Council on Aging, National Urban League, National Council of Senior Citizens, Green Thumb, Inc., and Asociacion Nacional pro Personas Mayores.

8.   Although trade unions have generally been much opposed to the spread of alternative work schedules, part-time work included, there is evidence that their position is loosening somewhat in this regard (Appelbaum and Gregory 1988, 1990; Carre, duRivage, and Tilly 1995). While unionization is minimal among part-time workers at present and virtually nonexistent among contract and temporary employees, the growth area for unions in the future is in the service sector, where the overwhelming majority of low-income, elder part-time workers are now and will continue to be employed. Consequently it behooves job-placement agencies at both the local and national levels, and national organizations advocating on behalf of elder workers, to actively begin exploration with unions about common interests and useful strategies to prevent further deterioration of part-time employment. This kind of exploration was not being actively pursued by study placement agencies at the time of our research.

Epilogue

Part-time employment has emerged as crucial in the lives of a large proportion of the elders participating in this research. Older adults in our research appeared to savor the opportunity provided by the job programs which placed them and the employers who hired them. Some appeared so grateful to have a job that they dared not complain about inadequacies in salary and fringe benefits or occurrences of discrimination in the work setting. In fact, few elders appeared to be particularly selective consumers in terms of the job-seeking process.

The potential of part-time employment for the older adult is undeniable. Yet abuses can easily enter into the equation. Everyone involved in the employment process—placement agency, employee, and employer—needs to understand that employing older workers is broadly beneficial. Employers benefit because they have eager, dependable, and competent workers who are grateful for the chance to work. Employees benefit for financial and social reasons. Society benefits by keeping a segment of the older population from sinking into poverty. Part-time employment, whether subsidized or not, should not be viewed as another attempt to support the elderly, but rather as a means of helping the elderly support themselves, at the same time that the economy and the very fabric of society are strengthened.

References

Allin, Susan, and Paul T. Decker. *Experimental Training Projects for Older Workers.* Washington, DC: Mathematica Policy Research, Inc., 1994.

"Alternatives to Downsizing." *Working Age* (July/August 1994): 2–3.

American Association of Retired Persons. *Work and Retirement: Employees Over 40 and Their Views.* Washington, DC: American Association of Retired Persons, 1986.

————. *Business and Older Workers: Current Perceptions and New Directions for the 1990s.* Washington, DC: AARP, 1989.

Anderson, Kathryn, Richard Burkhauser, and George Slotsve. "A Two Decade Comparison of Work after Retirement in the United States." *Geneva Papers on Risk and Insurance* 17 (January 1992): 26–39.

Appelbaum, Eileen. "Introduction. Structural Changes and the Growth of Part-Time and Temporary Employment." In *Part-Time and Temporary Employment,"* ed. Virginia L. duRivage, 1–14. Armonk, NY: M.E. Sharpe, 1992a.

————. "What's Driving the Growth of Contingent Employment?" In *New Policies for Part-Time and Contingent Workers,* ed. New Ways to Work, 9–11. San Francisco, CA: New Ways to Work, 1992b.

Appelbaum, Eileen, and Judith Gregory. "Union Responses to Contingent Work: Are Win-Win Outcomes Possible?" In *Flexible Workstyles: A Look at Contingent Labor,* eds. Kathleen Christensen and Mary Murphree, 69–75. Washington, DC: U.S. Department of Labor, Women's Bureau, Conference Summary, 1988.

————. "Flexible Employment: Union Perspectives." In *Bridges to Retirement,* ed. Peter Doeringer, 130–45. Ithaca, NY: ILR Press, School of Industrial and Labor Relations, Cornell University, 1990.

Ashbaugh, Donald L., and Charles H. Fay. "The Threshold for Aging in the Workplace." *Research on Aging* 9 (1987): 417–27.

Avolio, B., and D. Waldman. "Ratings of Managerial Skill Requirements: Comparison of Age-related and Job-related Factors." *Psychology and Aging* 4 (1989): 464–70.

Bales, S. N. "Fragments of Time: The Perils of Part-Time Work." *OWL Observer* 1 (January/February 1989): 8.

Barker, Kathleen. "Changing Assumptions and Contingent Solutions: The Costs and Benefits of Women Working Full- and Part-Time." *Sex Roles* (1993): 47–71.

Barth, Michael C., William McNaught, and Philip Rizzi. "Corporations and the Aging Workforce." In *Building the Competitive Workforce: Investing in Human Capital for Corporate Success,* ed. Philip H. Mirvis, 156–200. NY: John Wiley & Sons, 1993.

————. "Older Americans as Workers." In *Older and Active: How Americans Over 55 Are Contributing to Society,* ed. Scott A. Bass, 35–70. New Haven, CT: Yale University Press, 1995.

Bass, Scott A., ed. *Older and Active: How Americans Over 55 Are Contributing to Society.* New Haven, CT: Yale University Press, 1995.

Bass, Scott A., Frances A. Caro, and Yung-Ping Chen, eds. *Achieving a Productive Aging Society*. Westport, CT: Auburn House, 1993.

Bass, Scott A., Joseph F. Quinn, and Richard V. Burkhauser. "Toward Pro-Work Policies and Programs for Older Americans." In *Older and Active: How Americans Over 55 Are Contributing to Society*, ed. Scott A. Bass, 263–94. New Haven, CT: Yale University Press, 1995.

Belous, Richard S. "How Human Resource Systems Adjust to the Shift toward Contingent Workers." *Monthly Labor Review* 112 (1989a): 7–12.

———. *The Contingent Economy: The Growth of the Temporary, Part-Time, and Subcontracted Workforce*. Washington, DC: National Planning Association, 1989b.

Berkowitz, Monroe. "Functioning Ability and Job Performance as Workers Age." In *The Older Worker*, eds. Michael E. Borus, Herbert S. Parnes, Steven H. Sandell, and Bert Seidman, 87–114. Madison, WI: Industrial Relations Research Association, 1988.

Bessey, Barbara L., and Amanda M. Srijati. "Age Discrimination in Employment: An Interdisciplinary Review of the ADEA." *Research on Aging* 13 (December 1991): 413–57.

Blank, Rebecca M. "The Role of Part-Time Work in Women's Labor Market Choices Over Time." *American Economic Review* 79 (May 1989): 295–99.

———. "Are Part-Time Jobs Bad Jobs?" In *A Future of Lousy Jobs? The Changing Structure of U.S. Wages*, ed. Gary Burtless, 476–84. Washington, DC: The Brookings Institution, 1990.

———. "The Dynamics of Part-Time Work." Working Paper No. 4911. Cambridge, MA: NBER, November 1994.

———. "Contingent Work in a Changing Labor Market." In *Contingent Work in a Changing Labor Market: Labor Market Policies and Low-Skilled Workers*, eds. Richard B. Freeman and Peter Gottschalk. New York: Russell Sage, 1997.

Burkhauser, Richard V., and Joseph F. Quinn. "Labor Force Participation of Older Workers." Paper No. 20. Washington, DC: U.S. Department of Labor, Commission on Workforce Quality and Labor Market Efficiency, 1989.

———. "Changing Policy Signals." In *Age and Structural Lag: Society's Failure to Provide Meaningful Opportunities in Work, Family, and Leisure*, eds. Matilda White Riley, Robert L. Kahn, and Anne Foner, 237–62. NY: John Wiley & Sons, 1994.

Calasanti, Toni M., and Alessandro Bonanno. "Work 'Overtime': Economic Restructuring and the Retirement of a Class." *Sociological Quarterly* 33 (1992): 135–52.

Callaghan, Polly, and Heidi Hartmann. *Contingent Work: A Chart Book on Part-Time and Temporary Employment*. Washington, DC: Economic Policy Institute, 1991.

Carnevale, Anthony P., and Susan Carol Stone. "Developing the New Competitive Workforce." In *Aging and Competition: Rebuilding the U.S. Workforce*, eds. James A. Auerbach and Joyce C. Welsh, 94–144. Washington, DC: National Planning Association, 1994.

Carr, Darrell E. "Overtime Work: An Expanded View." *Monthly Labor Review* 109 (November 1986): 36–39.

Carre, Francoise J. "Temporary Employment in the Eighties." In *New Policies for the Part-Time and Contingent Workforce*, ed. Virginia L. duRivage, 45–87. Armonk, NY: M.E. Sharpe, 1992.

Carre, Francoise J., Virginia duRivage, and Chris Tilly. "Piecing Together the Fragmented Workplace: Unions and Public Policy on Flexible Employment." In *Unions and Public Policy*, ed. Lawrence G. Flood. Westport, CT: Greenwood Press, 1995.

Castro, Janice. "Disposable Workers." *Time*, 29 March 1993, 43–47.

Centaur Associates, Inc. *Evaluation Study of the Senior Community Service Employment Program Funded under Title V of the Older Americans Act*. Washington, DC: Centaur Associates, 1986.

Christensen, Kathleen. "Bridges over Troubled Waters: How Older Workers View the

Labor Market." In *Bridges to Retirement*, ed. Peter Doeringer, 175–208. Ithaca, NY: ILR Press, School of Industrial and Labor Relations, Cornell University, 1990.

Christensen, Kathleen, and Mary Murphree, eds. *Flexible Workstyles: A Look at Contingent Labor.* Washington, DC: U.S. Department of Labor, Women's Bureau, Conference Summary, 1988.

Christensen, Kathleen, Helen Axel, Dean Hewitt, and Thomas Nardone. "Protecting Older Contingent Workers." In *New Policies for Part-Time and Contingent Workers*, ed. New Ways To Work, 42–45. San Francisco, CA: New Ways To Work, 1992.

Commonwealth Fund. Commission on Elderly People Living Alone. *Old, Alone and Poor.* Baltimore, MD: Commonwealth Fund, 1987.

———. "News Release: Case Studies at Major Corporations Show Why Employing Workers Over 50 Makes Good Business Sense." NY: Commonwealth Fund, 21 May 1991.

———. *The Untapped Resource: The Final Report of the Americans Over 55 at Work Program.* NY: Commonwealth Fund, November 1993.

Cox, Enid O. "Older Worker Issues and Program Strategies: SCSEP Administrators' Perspective." Arlington, VA: DTI, 31 January 1995.

Davis, Karen. *Life Satisfaction and Older Adults.* Americans Over 55 at Work Program. Background Paper No. 6. NY: Commonwealth Fund, 1991.

Deets, Horace B. "Job Program that Helps Now Needs Help Itself." *AARP Bulletin* 36 (March 1995): 3.

Doeringer, Peter B., ed. *Bridges to Retirement.* Ithaca, NY: ILR Press, School of Industrial and Labor Relations, Cornell University, 1990a.

———. "Economic Security, Labor Market Flexibility, and Bridges to Retirement." In *Bridges to Retirement*, ed. Peter Doeringer, 3–19. Ithaca, NY: ILR Press, School of Industrial and Labor Relations, Cornell University, 1990b.

Dooley, Alberta Coy. "Senior Community Service Employment Programs: The Older Worker Perspective." Arlington, VA: DTI, 31 January 1995.

Duke University, Center for the Study of Aging and Human Development. *Multidimensional Functional Assessment: The OARS Methodology.* 2nd ed. Durham, NC: Duke University, 1978.

duRivage, Virginia L., ed. *New Policies for the Part-Time and Contingent Workforce.* Armonk, NY: M.E. Sharpe, 1992.

Federal Register. 19 July 1985, p. 29613.

Ferman, Louis A., M. Hoyman, J. Cutcher-Gersenfied, and E. Savoie, eds. *New Developments in Worker Training.* Madison, WI: Industrial Relations Research Association, 1990.

Fierman, Jaclyn. "The Contingency Work Force." *Fortune* 129 (24 January 1994): 30–36.

Foster, Susan E., and Jack A. Brizius. "Caring Too Much? American Women and the Nation's Caregiving Crisis." In *Women on the Front Lines: Meeting the Challenge of an Aging America*, eds. Jessie Allen and Alan Pifer, 47–73. Washington, DC: Urban Institute Press, 1993.

Freedman, Marc. *Seniors in National and Community Service: A Report Prepared for the Commonwealth Fund's Americans Over 55 at Work Program.* Philadelphia, PA: Public/Private Ventures, April 1994.

Fretz, Burton D., Vicki Gottlich, and Shannon Schmoyer. "Older Women and Income Security." *Clearinghouse Review* 25 (1991): 453–66.

Friedman, Barry L. "Job Prospects for Mature Workers." *Journal of Aging and Social Policy* 4 (1992): 53–72.

Friedmann, Eugene A., and Robert J. Havighurst. *The Meaning of Work and Retirement.* Chicago, IL: University of Chicago Press, 1954.

Garcia, Alejandro. "An Examination of the Economic Support Systems of Elderly Hispanics." In *Hispanic Elderly: A Cultural Signature*, ed. Marta Sotomayor, 227–47. Edinburg, TX: Pan American University Press, 1988.

———. "Income Security and Elderly Latinos." In *Elderly Latinos: Issues and Solutions* for the 21st Century, ed. Marta Sotomayor and Alejandro Garcia, 17–28. Washington, DC: National Hispanic Council on Aging, 1993.

General Accounting Office. *Workers at Risk: Increased Numbers in Contingent Employment Lack Insurance, Other Benefits.* Washington, DC: General Accounting Office, March 1991.

Golden, Lonnie. "Employment and Marginalization of Older Workers in the United States." In *Working Part-Time: Risks and Opportunities,* eds. Barbara B. Warme, Katherina L.P. Lundy, and Larry A. Lundy, 205–23. NY: Praeger Publishing, 1992.

Gollub, J.O. *Emerging Employment Opportunities for Older Workers: Practice and Potential.* Washington, DC: National Commission for Employment Policy, 1983.

Goodwin, Leonard. *Do the Poor Really Want to Work? A Social-Psychological Study of Work Orientations.* Washington, DC: Brookings Institution, 1972.

Hardy, Melissa A. "Employment after Retirement: Who Gets Back In?" *Research on Aging* 13 (September 1991): 267–88.

Haywood, Mark D., Melissa A. Hardy, and Mei-Chun Liu. "Work after Retirement: The Experiences of Older Men in the United States." *Social Science Research* 23 (1994): 82–107.

Henretta, John C. "Social Structures and Age-Based Careers." In *Age and Structural Lag: Society's Failure to Provide Meaningful Opportunities in Work, Family, and Leisure,* eds. Matilda White Riley, Robert L. Kahn, and Anne Foner, 57–79. NY: John Wiley & Sons, 1994.

Herz, Diane E. "Employment Characteristics of Older Women, 1987." *Monthly Labor Review* 11 (1988): 3–12.

———. "Work after Early Retirement: An Increasing Trend among Men." *Monthly Labor Review* 118 (April 1995): 13–20.

Herz, Diane E., and Philip L. Rones. "Barriers to Employment of Older Workers." *Monthly Labor Review* 112 (1989): 14–21.

Hirshorn, Barbara A., and Dennis T. Hoyer. "Private Sector Hiring and Use of Retirees: The Firm's Perspective." *The Gerontologist* 34 (1994): 50–58.

Holstein, Martha. "Productive Aging: A Feminist Critique." *Journal of Aging and Social Policy* 4(1992): 17–34.

Horvath, Francis W. "The Pulse of Economic Change: Displaced Workers of 1981–85." *Monthly Labor Review* 110 (June 1987): 3–12.

Iams, Howard M. "Jobs of Persons Working after Receiving Retired-Worker Benefits." *Social Security Bulletin* 50 (1987): 4–18.

Ichniowski, Bernard, and Anne E. Preston. "New Trends in Part-Time Employment." Proceedings of the Thirty-Eighth Annual Meeting of the Industrial Relations Research Association, 1985.

International Labor Office. "Part-Time Work." *Conditions of Work Digest* 8 (1989): entire issue.

Irelan, Lola M., William Rabin, and Karen Schwab. *Social Security Administration Retirement History Study.* Vol. II, *Technical Description.* Washington, DC: U.S. Department of Health and Human Services, Social Security Administration, Office of Policy, 1987. SSA Publication No. 13–11783.

Jencks, Christopher, Lauri Perman, and Lee Rainwater. "What Is a Good Job? A New Measure of Labor Market Success." *American Journal of Sociology* 93 (1988): 1322–57.

Jondrow, Jim, Frank Brechling, and Alan Marcus. "Older Workers in the Market for Part-Time Employment." In *The Problem Isn't Age,* ed. Steven H. Sandell, 84–99. NY: Praeger Publishers, 1987.

Kahn, Robert L. "Opportunities, Aspirations, and Goodness of Fit." In *Age and Structural Lag: Society's Failure to Provide Meaningful Opportunities in Work, Family, and Leisure,* ed. Matilda White Riley, Robert L. Kahn, and Anne Foner, 37–53. NY: John Wiley & Sons, 1994.

Kahne, Hilda. *Reconceiving Part-Time Work.* Totowa, NJ: Rowman and Allanheld, 1985.

———. "Part-Time Work: A Positive Case." In *Proceedings of the Thirty-Eighth Annual*

Meeting of the Industrial Relations Research Association. Madison, WI: Industrial Relations Research Association, 1986.

——. "Part-Time Work: A Hope and a Peril." In *Working Part-Time: Risks and Opportunities,* eds. Barbara B. Warme, Katherina L. Lundy, and Larry A. Lundy, 295–309. NY: Praeger Publishing, 1992.

——. "Part-Time Work: "A Reassessment for a Changing Economy." *Social Service Review* 68 (1994): 417–36.

Karasek, Robert, and Tores Theorell. *Healthy Work: Stress, Productivity, and the Reconstruction of Working Life.* NY: Basic Books, 1990.

Kaye, Lenard W., and Leslie B. Alexander. "Perceived Job Discrimination among Lower-Income Elderly Part-Timers." *Journal of Gerontological Social Work* 23 (1995): 99–121.

Kilborn, Peter T. "Threat to Job Program for the Elderly Poor." *New York Times,* 15 September 1995, A16.

——. "For Elderly Just Hanging On, Oasis of Jobs, but Shrinking." *New York Times,* 1 September 1990, A1, A7.

Kramer, Natalie. "Employee Benefits for Older Americans." *Monthly Labor Review* 118 (April 1995): 21–27.

Kronick, Jane C., and Leslie B. Alexander. "The Older Woman in the Workforce." Paper presented to the U.S. Department of Education. Contract #433JAH2RE406. April 1993.

Kuriansky, Joan, and Diana Porter. Improving Employment Opportunities for Older Women: Report by the Older Women's League, forthcoming.

Lehrmann, Eugene. "SCSEP: A Model Employment Program Worth Keeping." *Highlights* 13 (July–August 1995): 2.

Levitan, Sar A., and Elizabeth A. Conway. "Part-timers: Living on Half-rations." *Challenge* 31 (1988): 9–16.

Lewis, Robert. "More Elderly Retirees Find the Going Rough." *AARP Bulletin* 35 (May 1994): 1, 14.

Louis Harris and Associates. *Aging in the Eighties: America in Transition.* Washington, DC: National Council on Aging, 1981.

——. *Labor Force 2000.* Study No. 902062. NY: Louis Harris & Associates, 1991.

——. *Productive Aging: A Survey of Americans Age 55 and Over.* Study No. 902061. NY: Louis Harris & Associates, April 1992.

McEvoy, George M., and William F. Cascio. "Cumulative Evidence of the Relationship between Employee Age and Job Performance." *Journal of Applied Psychology* 74 (1989): 11–17.

McNaught, William. "Realizing the Potential: Some Examples." In *Age and Structural Lag: Society's Failure to Provide Meaningful Opportunities in Work, Family, and Leisure,* eds. Matilda White Riley, Robert L. Kahn, and Anne Foner, 219–36. NY: John Wiley & Sons, 1994.

McNaught, William, and Michael C. Barth. "Are Older Workers 'Good Buys'? A Case Study of Days Inns of America." *Sloan Management Review* 33 (1992): 53–63.

Malveaux, Julianne. "Resiliency amidst Inequality: Older Women Workers in an Aging Society." In *Women on the Front Lines: Meeting the Challenge of an Aging America,* eds. Jessie Allen and Alan Pifer, 133–66. Washington, DC: Urban Institute Press, 1993.

Medoff, James. "Middle-Aged and Out-of-Work." Democratic Study Center Report Series. Washington, DC: Democratic Study Center, April 15, 1993.

Meier, Elizabeth S. "Managing an Older Work Force." In *The Older Worker,* eds. Michael E. Borus, Herbert S. Parnes, Steven H. Sandell, and Bert Seidman, 167–89. Madison, WI: Industrial Relations Research Association, 1988.

Meister, D. "Part-timers Are Second-class Workers." *Philadelphia Inquirer,* 21 January 1988, 21-A.

Mirkin, B. A. "Early Retirement as a Labor Force Policy." *Monthly Labor Review* 110 (1987): 19–33.

Mitchell, Olivia S. "Pensions and Older Workers." In *The Older Worker*, ed. Michael E. Borus, Herbert S. Parnes, Steven H. Sandell, and Bert Seidman, 151–66. Madison, WI: Industrial Relations Research Association, 1988.

Moen, Phyllis. "Women, Work, and Family: A Sociological Perspective on Changing Roles." In *Age and Structural Lag: Society's Failure to Provide Meaningful Opportunities in Work, Family, and Leisure*, eds. Matilda White Riley, Robert L. Kahn, and Anne Foner, 151–70. NY: John Wiley & Sons, 1994.

Moen, Phyllis, and Ken R. Smith. "Women at Work: Commitment and Behavior over the Life Course." *Sociological Forum* 1 (1986): 450–75.

Monk, Abraham, Lenard W. Kaye, and Beverly Diamond. *A Survey Study of Elderly Residents at Brookdale Village*. NY: Brookdale Institute on Aging and Adult Human Development, Columbia University, 1986.

Morrison, Malcolm H. "Work and Retirement in an Older Society." In *Our Aging Society: Paradox and Promises*, eds. Alan Pifer and Lydia Bronte. NY: W. W. Norton & Co., 1986.

Murray, Carolyn B., Syed Khatib, and Maurice Jackson. "Social Indices and the Black Elderly: A Comparative Life Cycle Approach to the Study of Double Jeopardy." In *Black Adult Development and Aging*, ed. Reginald L. Jones, 167–87. Berkeley, CA: Cobb & Henry Publishers, 1989.

Myers, Daniel A. "Work after Cessation of a Career Job." *Journal of Gerontology* 46 (1991): 93–102.

National Caucus and Center on Black Aged, Inc. *Job Placement Systems for Older Workers*. Washington, DC: National Caucus and Center on Black Aged, Inc., 1987.

———. *Health Status of Aged Blacks*. Washington, DC: National Caucus and Center on Black Aged, Inc., December 1992.

———. *A Profile of Elderly Blacks*. Washington, DC: NCCBA, August 1994.

National Commission for Employment Policy. *Older Workers: Prospects, Problems and Policies*. 9th Annual Report. Washington, DC: NCEP, 1985.

National Commission on Working Women of Wider Opportunities for Women. *Women, Work and Age*. Washington, DC: National Commission on Working Women of Wider Opportunities for Women, 1987.

National Institute on Aging. "Survey Sketches New Portrait of Aging America." *News Release*, 17 June 1993.

New Ways to Work. *New Policies for Part-Time and Contingent Workers*. San Francisco, CA: New Ways to Work, 1992.

9 to 5, National Association of Working Women. *Working at the Margins: Part-Time and Temporary Workers in the United States*. Cleveland, OH, 1986.

———. *Social Insecurity: The Economic Marginalization of Older Workers*. Cleveland, OH, 1987.

Olmsted, Barney. "The Ifs, Ands and Buts of Job Sharing for Older Workers." Paper presented at the Grant Makers in Aging Meeting, Memphis, Tennessee, 1985.

Olmsted, Barney, and Suzanne Smith. *Creating a Flexible Workplace: How to Select and Manage Alternative Work Options*. NY: American Management Association, 1989.

———. *Creating a Flexible Workplace*. 2nd ed. NY: American Management Association, 1994.

Olmsted, Barney, and Stephen Trippe. "The Flexible Workplace: Implications for State Employment Policy and Regulations." In *Excellence at Work: Policy Option Papers for the National Governors' Association*, ed. Evelyn Ganzglass, 111–50. Kalamazoo, MI: W.E. Upjohn Institute for Employment Research, 1992.

Parker, Robert E. *Flesh Peddlers and Warm Bodies: The Temporary Help Industry and Its Workers*. New Brunswick, NJ: Rutgers University Press, 1994.

Parnes, Herbert S., and David G. Summers. "Shunning Retirement: Work Experiences of Men in Their Seventies and Early Eighties." *Journal of Gerontology* 49 (1994): 5117–24.

Peterson, David A., and Pamela F. Wendt. "Training and Education of Older Americans as Workers and Volunteers." In *Older and Active: How Americans over 55 Are Contributing to Society*, ed. Scott A. Bass, 217–36. New Haven, CT: Yale University Press, 1995.

Pisarski, A.E. *Commuting in America: A National Report on Commuting Patterns and Trends*. Westport, CT: END Foundation for Transportation, 1987.

Plewes, Thomas J. "Understanding the Data on Part-Time and Temporary Employment." In *Flexible Workstyles: A Look at Contingent Labor*, eds. Kathleen Christensen and Mary Murphree, 9–13. Washington, DC: U.S. Department of Labor, Women's Bureau, Conference Summary, 1988.

Polivka, Anne E., and Thomas Nardone. "On the Definition of Contingent Work." *Monthly Labor Review* 112 (1989): 9–16.

Porter, Allison. "The Path to Poverty: An Analysis of Women's Retirement Income." Washington, DC: Older Women's League, April 1995.

Quinn, Joseph F., and Richard V. Burkhauser. "Work and Retirement." In *Handbook of Aging and the Social Services*. 3rd ed., eds. Robert H. Binstock and Linda K. George, 307–27. NY: Van Nostrand Reinhold, 1990.

Quinn, Robert P., and Graham L. Staines. *The 1977 Quality of Employment Survey*. Ann Arbor, MI: Institute for Social Research, University of Michigan, 1979.

Rayman, Paula, Kimberly Allshouse, and Jessie Allen. "Resiliency amidst Inequity: Older Women Workers in an Aging United States." In *Women on the Front Lines: Meeting the Challenge of an Aging America*, eds. Jessie Allen and Alan Pifer, 133–66. Washington, DC: Urban Institute Press, 1993.

Rebitzer, James, and Lowell Taylor. "A Model of Dual Labor Markets with Uncertain Product Demand." University of Texas at Austin, Department of Economics, July 1988. Mimeo.

Rix, Sarah E. *Older Workers*. Santa Barbara, CA: ABC-CLIO, 1990.

Robinson, P.K., Sally Coberly, and Carolyn Paul. "Work and Retirement." In *Handbook of Aging and the Social Services*, 2nd ed., eds. Robert H. Binstock and Ethel Shanas. NY: Van Nostrand Reinhold, 1985.

Rosen, Benson, and Thomas H. Jerdee. "The Persistence of Age and Sex Stereotypes in the 1990s: The Influence of Age and Gender in Management Decisions." AARP Public Policy Institute, Issue Brief No. 22, March 1995.

Rosenthal, Neal H. "More than Wages at Issue in Job Quality Debate." *Monthly Labor Review* 12 (1989): 4.

Ruhm, Christopher J. "Career Jobs, Bridge Employment, and Retirement." In *Bridges to Retirement*, ed. Peter Doeringer, 92–107. Ithaca, NY: ILR Press, School of Industrial and Labor Relations, Cornell University, 1990.

Saltford, Nancy, and Sarah Snider. "Characteristics of the Part-Time Work Force." EBRI Special Report SR-22. EBRI Issue Brief No. 149. Washington, DC: EBRI, May 1994.

Sandell, Steven H. "Public Policies and Programs Affecting Older Workers." In *The Older Worker*, eds. Michael E. Borus, Herbert S. Parnes, Steven H. Sandell, and Bert Seidman, 207–28. Madison, WI: Industrial Relations Research Association, 1988.

Schrank, Harris T., and Joan M. Waring. "Older Workers: Ambivalence and Interventions." *The Annals*, AAPSS 503 (1989): 113–26.

Schultz, James H., Allan Borowski, and William H. Crown. *The Economics of Population Aging: The "Graying" of Australia, Japan, and the United States*. NY: Auburn House, 1991.

Shapiro, Evelyn, and Noralou P. Roos. "Retired and Employed Elderly Persons: Their Utilization of Health Care Services." *The Gerontologist* 22 (1982): 187–93.

Shaw, Lois B. "Special Problems of Older Women Workers." In *The Older Worker*, eds. Michael E. Borus, Herbert S. Parnes, Steven H. Sandell, and Bert Seidman, 55–86. Madison, WI: Industrial Relations Research Association, 1988.

Sicker, Martin. "The Changing Work Environment: Implications for Midlife and Older

Workers." Washington, DC: American Association of Retired Persons, Work Force Program Department, February 1994. Unpublished paper.

Siegel, Jacob S. *A Generation of Change: A Profile of America's Older Population.* NY: Russell Sage, 1993.

Sotomayor, Marta. "The Latino Elderly: A Policy Agenda." In *Elderly Latinos: Issues and Solutions for the 21st Century*, eds. Marta Sotomayor and Alejandro Garcia, 1–16. Washington, DC: National Hispanic Council on Aging, 1993.

Sotomayor, Marta, and Susan Randolph. "The Health Status of the Hispanic Elderly." In *Hispanic Elderly: A Cultural Signature*, ed. Marta Sotomayor, 137–60. Edinburg, TX: Pan American University Press, 1988.

Soumerai, Stephen B., and Jerry Avorn. "Perceived Health, Life Satisfaction, and Activity in Urban Elderly: A Controlled Study of the Impact of Part-Time Work." *Journal of Gerontology* 38 (1983): 356–62.

Sterns, Harvey L., and M.A. McDaniel. *Job Performance and the Older Worker.* Washington, DC: Public Policy Institute. American Association of Retired Persons, 1994.

Sterns, Harvey L., and Suzanne M. Miklos, "The Aged Worker in a Changing Environment." *Journal of Vocational Behavior*, 47 (December 1995): 248–68.

Sterns, Harvey L., and Anthony A. Sterns. "Age, Health and Employment Capability of Older Americans." In *Aging and Active: Dimensions of Productive Engagement among Older Americans*, eds. Scott A. Bass, Michael Barth, Philip Rizzi, and William McNaught, 10–34. New Haven, CT: Yale University Press, 1995.

Sticker, Martin. "The Changing Work Environment: Implications for Midlife and Older Workers." AARP, Work Force Programs Department, Internal Document, February 1994.

Stone, Robyn, Gail Lee Cafferata, and Judith Sangl. "Caregivers of the Frail Elderly: A National Profile." *The Gerontologist* 27 (1987): 616–26.

Sum, Andrew M., and W. Neal Fogg. "Labor Market and Poverty Problems of Older Workers and Their Families." In *Bridges to Retirement*, ed. Peter Doeringer, 64–91. Ithaca, NY: ILR Press, School of Industrial and Labor Relations, Cornell University, 1990.

Tilly, Chris. *Short Hours, Short Shrift: Causes and Consequences of Part-Time Work.* Washington, DC: Economic Policy Institute, 1990.

———. "Two Faces of Part-Time Work." In *Part-Time Work: Opportunity or Dead End?*, eds. Katherina L. P. Lundy and Barbara B. Warme, 227–38. New York, NY: Praeger, 1992a.

———. "Short Hours, Short Shrift: Causes and Consequences of Part-Time Work." In *New Policies for the Part-Time and Contingent Workforce*, ed. Virginia L. duRivage, 15–44. Armonk, NY: M.E. Sharpe, 1992b.

———. *Half a Job. Bad and Good Part-Time Jobs in a Changing Labor Market.* Philadelphia: Temple University Press, 1996.

Uchitelle, Louis. "Retirement's Worried Face." *New York Times*, 30 July 1995, Section 3, 1, 4–5.

U.S. Bureau of Labor Statistics. Monthly. *Employment and Earnings*, January 1994.

U.S. Department of Health and Human Services. *Healthy People 2000.* DHHS Publication No. (PHS) 91–50213. Washington, DC: U.S. Government Printing Office, 1990.

Useem, Michael. "The Impact of American Business Restructuring on Older Workers." *Perspectives on Aging* 22 (October–December 1993): 12–15.

———. "Business Restructuring and the Aging Workforce." *Looking Ahead* 16 (January 1995): 16–22.

Warme, Barbara D., Katherina L. Lundy, and Larry A. Lundy, "Introduction." In *Working Part-Time: Risks and Opportunities*, eds. Barbara D. Warme, Katherina Lundy, and Larry A. Lundy, 11–17. NY: Praeger Publishing, 1992

Weiss, Francine K. *Employment Discrimination against Older Women: A Handbook on*

Litigating Age and Sex Discrimination Cases. Washington, DC: Older Women's League, 1989.

"Why Support SCSEP? It Works!" *Highlights* 13 (July–August 1995): 3.

Woodbury, Stephen A. "Current Economic Issues in Employee Benefits." Paper No. 39. U.S. Department of Labor Commission on Workforce Quality and Labor Market Efficiency, Washington, DC, 1989.

Wright, Mark. Manager of Communication and Membership Services, Association for Commuter Transportation, Washington, DC. Interview by Leslie Alexander, 22 October 1990.

Yankelovitch, Skelly, and White, Inc. *Workers Over 50: Old Myths, New Realities.* Washington, DC: American Association of Retired Persons, 1985.

Index